Escape from Ugly Mom Island!

The Ultimate Mom Style Guide

by

Holly Hester

Illustrations by Bill Shortridge

Praise for *"Escape from Ugly Mom Island!"*

by Holly Hester

"If you love to laugh and are a mom, know a mom, or have had a mom, then this is the book for you! I haven't been interested in fashion since I protested the uncomfortable one-piece gym suits we were forced to wear in junior high, but I found myself mentally putting together cute ensembles from this helpful book. The pictures are beautiful. The advice useful and witty. Buy this book!"

- Miriam Trogdon, *Consulting Producer, Last Man Standing*

"It's like a classic Cinderella story... if Cindy started out in stone-washed mom jeans with three kids wiping dirt and boogers on her clothes. I giggled, I flinched, I learned a little and I enjoyed the whole darn thing!"

- Joules, *PocketfulofJoules.com*

"Look, there are a lot of fashion advice books and workshops and magazine articles and blogs out there (even I have one). But none of them is half as entertaining to read as this one, and I've read Cristina Ferrare's seminal 1984 masterwork, Style. And unlike many advice givers (cough cough, Gwyneth), Holly has actually been to Ugly Mom Island. She figured out how to escape and now she can help you escape, too. Throw out those gigantic white sneakers (you know the ones I'm talking about) and get started already!"

- Heidi, *FranticbutFabulous.com*

"I love this book! The illustrations are perfect. It was so fun and easy to read. I clung to every word. I've never read anything like it before and my mind is still curious about all the cavernous vaginas out there…"

- Bo, *veterinarian*

For moms everywhere. *I totally get it.*

Contents

Introduction

Chapter 1 - Who is this book for? 1

Chapter 2 - Why would you ever take advice from me? 3

Chapter 3 - Why pick a style? 7

Chapter 4 – Rock & Roll 11

Chapter 5 – Euro 23

Chapter 6 – Slacker Mom 39

Chapter 7 – Classic 46

Chapter 8 – Sporty Chic 58

Chapter 9 – Mod 69

Chapter 10 – Artsy Mom 85

Chapter 11 – Gamine 93

Chapter 12 – Hippie 104

Chapter 13 – Bombshell 119

Chapter 14 – The 3 B's Buying, Budget and Butts 131

Chapter 15 - The Ten Commandments of Mom Fashion 133

Chapter 16 - The New You 136

Introduction

Thank you for buying my book. I know you could have selected a lot of other books, great pieces of literature, in fact, but I think you'll find this book is better than *The Great Gatsby* or *Anna Karenina*. And not because it's better written. Trust me, it's definitely not. But because it will make a bigger change in your life than any *Moby-Dick* ever will. By selecting my silly little book on mom clothes, you have taken the most important step in your road to fashion recovery --

Admitting you dress like a mom.

I don't know of any occupation that is harder to dress for than the job of mom. Do accountants get barfed on for years on end? Do plumbers go without sleep constantly and have no time to even shower? Does society expect anyone else who has gone through a traumatizing medical event (like giving birth) to bounce back instantly as if it never happened? *Wow, have you seen Grace? She was in a car accident three months ago and she is still limping. And seriously, what's up with those pins in her knees? OMG, she should really do some Pilates and get a haircut...*

And yet, along with our new babies, every mom gets a heaping helping of criticism and unrealistic expectations. Over time, this makes us feel like total failures and we lose our self-esteem, which, along with our previously normal-sized vaginas, never returns.

So yeah, this is more than just a book about clothes. And judging by what you've just read, obviously not a great piece of literature, but a sure fire way to a happier, more fabulous you. I promise. Cross my heart and hope to go to Chuck E. Cheese. (Which, to me, is worse than dying.)

Holly

Chapter 1

Who is This Book For?

Although I reference moms with young children a lot, this book is not just for them. I've written this book for anyone who wants to finally grab that brass ring of fashion.

Here are some people that might enjoy my book:

1. Anyone who was voted "Best Dressed" in high school as a prank.

2. Anyone who has ever uttered the phrase, "The cat just puked on my tube top."

3. Anyone with a mullet haircut that's not a Halloween wig.

4. Anyone who thinks a jog bra is "almost like a shirt."

5. Anyone who has ever Googled, "Bedazzler clubs in my area."

6. Anyone who has grown confused over the role pajamas play in everyday life.

7. Anyone who longs for the "stone-washed days."

8. Anyone who has ever worn a Christmas sweater with a battery insert.

9. Anyone whose big white sneakers can be seen from space.

10. Anyone who wears a self-describing t-shirt as in, "I'm just a crazy bitch."

This book makes a great gift, but only for that special someone in your life who has *verbally expressed an interest* in looking better. This book is not to be given as a wake up call to anyone who frequently appears on the *People of Walmart* website because they think they have great style.

In which case, this book could end a friendship.

Chapter 2

Why Would You Ever Take Advice From Me?

Here's what I'm not:

A fashion expert, a celebrity mom, a stylist that *dresses* a celebrity mom, a person who works in the fashion industry, a person who's obsessed with the fashion industry, someone who spends a ton of money and time on clothes or anyone who should probably be giving fashion advice at all.

Here's what I am:

A mom who used to look terrible and now I don't.

Let me explain. But in order to do that, we need to go way back to the year 2003, before I had my first child. (I'm on my third now.) I had a cute little baby bump and I was so cocky, so confident that I would never turn into one of *those moms.* You know the mom I'm talking about -- the one with the pleated jeans, big white sneakers and overloaded backpack teeming with healthy snacks and not a shred of dignity. The mom who has given up all hope of ever looking fit for public consumption, whose frazzled expression and stained clothing I regarded as a cautionary tale of what I was going to avoid.

No, I was going to be a *celebrity mom.* I was going to look fabulous from the moment I made my grand exit from the hospital with my newborn perfectly matching my Manolos. And since I hadn't gained a single ounce during pregnancy, my casual, but chic yoga clothes would cling to my ass *better than ever...*

But I didn't become a celebrity mom. Being a mom was much more challenging than I expected and instead of channeling Gwyneth Paltrow, I looked more like a newly divorced gym teacher on a Lifetime movie. After having three kids in less than six years, my wardrobe dissolved into an uninterrupted series of baggy sweatpants, oversized t-shirts and big underwear. Motherhood took every single moment of my free time. Suddenly, a shower was a luxury and clothes shopping a definite fantasy.

I told myself this was all fine. I'm a mom now and this is how moms look. Nobody notices moms anyway, right? And who am I trying to impress? My husband is still desperate enough to have sex with me. My children use my clothes as a convenient napkin. Even that weird stay-at-home dad at the park checks me out once in a while. *So what's the problem?* It seemed like me as Ugly Mom was here to stay.

But I was ignoring a real problem. I was depressed and didn't know why. I would panic at the thought of having to dress up for a party because I didn't have the body or wardrobe to wear anything I felt good in. I'd forgotten who I'd been *before* I had kids and now I certainly didn't recognize the person I'd become in the rear view mirror of my minivan.

Then one night as I was changing to go out to dinner, my daughter grabbed an old bridesmaid dress from my closet and said, "Why don't you wear this?" I told her thanks, but no thanks. I think I'd be slightly overdressed for Chinese food in a floor length pink taffeta gown. But my daughter insisted. She shoved the dress into my arms and said, "Well, it's better than what you usually wear."

In Oprah-speak, this was my aha moment. *So I wasn't invisible.* People did notice how badly I was dressing. No wonder my kids wiped their noses on me. No wonder people ignored me. No wonder I felt so awful all the time. (The only thing I still wondered was why my husband continued to have sex with me. We're talking about some seriously low standards here.)

I actually wore the bridesmaid's dress to dinner and you know what? I felt better. I felt pretty. Of course, I didn't look pretty. I looked insane and I'm sure the people at the restaurant felt sorry for my husband and children. *But I felt better because I tried.* I had thrown my hat in the ring of fashion and I was ready to declare a fight.

That night I vowed to dress up every single day for a year – no exceptions. It didn't matter where I was going. As far as I was concerned, a trip to the grocery store was a trip down the runway. I chronicled my adventures in a blog called "My Year of Fabulous" and it not only turned out to be one of the best decisions I've ever made, but one of the best years of my life.

This book is all about that fashion experience and why I feel qualified to give you advice -- not because I've got a diploma on my wall from Coco Chanel University, but because I consider myself to be a fashion success story. Every single piece of advice I'm giving you is based on me guinea-pigging myself in the name of chic science. I know what a real mom goes through and therefore I will never, ever tell you that a pair of three-inch heels is the perfect thing to wear for pushing your kid on a swing at the park or a white dress can be worn for more than ten seconds without it looking like it's been in a playdough tsunami.

If this book was a war movie, Diane Von Furstenberg would play the highly decorated general who has never seen an ounce of blood and I would play the grizzled, fingerless, platoon leader who drinks too much and never obeys the rules, but knows exactly how to make you look great.

So whose advice would you rather follow when it comes to "Escaping from Ugly Mom Island"? The fashion experts or me?

Okay, the fashion experts. But hey, you already bought my book, so you might as well enjoy it!

Chapter 3

Why Pick a Style?

To be honest, even before having kids I really knew nothing about fashion. I've always worked as a sitcom writer, a group of people not exactly known for their style expertise. So when it came time to start putting outfits together every day, I was terrified. I studied tons of fashion magazines, but the clothes they suggested were either way too expensive or

just plain stupid-looking. Finally, I came across a wonderful book called *The Lucky Guide to Mastering any Style*. It explained in detail different types of styles and the clothes you needed in order to master each style. I loved this book because by breaking clothes into categories, fashion finally started to make sense to me. I began imagining fashion as a country and its cities were the different styles.

I decided the best way to find my own style was to try out a new style each month until I discovered one that fit my personality and lifestyle. But what I thought was going to be a practical experiment turned out to be more of a *sociological experiment*. I was shocked to find that people treated me completely differently based on what style I was wearing. Even people who knew me! It was the weirdest thing. Like schizophrenic weird. By the end of my style trial, I felt like I had ten different personalities.

- When I dressed in Euro, strangers would open doors for me.

- When I dressed in Rock & Roll, the sketchy crowd at the skate park suddenly liked me.

- When I dressed in Bombshell, men would hit on me.

- When I dressed in Hippie, I looked so young and carefree that someone thought my three-year-old son was my BROTHER.

- When I dressed in Classic, people would stop me on the street and ask for directions.

- When I dressed in Sporty Chic, kids at the park would ask me to play with them.

My clothes subconsciously instructed people how to treat me. I finally understood why me as Ugly Mom was ignored. I was sending out this massive Bat-signal to all of humanity. "Ignore me!" "I have nothing interesting to say!" "My tedious conversations about my children will bum you out!" "I smell like baby wipes!" By finding a style, I became someone to reckon with. Sure, I probably still smelled like baby wipes, but it didn't matter. I had changed everyone's minds as soon as I walked in the door.

Another wonderful thing about finding your style is that it makes shopping so much easier. Have you ever walked into a store and thought, "I need new clothes and I don't want to keep buying the same crap that I always buy, so W.T.F. do I get?" Then you buy like five things you'd never, ever wear and they sit in your closet forever. Style changes all that. You become like a shopping terminator, flipping through racks in seconds because you can identify exactly what you need.

After finding my style, I've even been able to shop *with my kids*, which has never happened before without ending in tantrums and tears. (Mostly on my part.) I just say to them things like, "I'm looking for a button-down denim shirt." And miraculously, they'll go find it! They're like sticky personal shoppers! Then once you get home and add the new items into your closet, you can put outfits together in seconds because everything matches.

In the next section of this book, you'll find ten styles that could possibly work for you. I give a detailed description of each style as well as an illustrated guide to the basic wardrobe you will need to rock a look. Also, I've included some of my blog posts so you can see how you might expect to be treated in each particular style.

But before we move to that section, I'm going to ask you to do a little soul searching. It's therapy time and I want you to think about you for a change. Not those loud, little creatures you obsess over every day. But you.

As Nina Garcia says, *"With style, you show the world who you are."* So, my question to you is –

Who are you?

You don't have to be really specific yet. Just think in general terms like, "I'm super smart" or "edgy" or "organized" or "creative". And if you're not too thrilled with who you currently are you can think of who you'd like to become. The sky is the limit on this one, so dream big. Think of things like, "I'm a world champion women's stand up paddle boarder" or "I fly my private jet to Paris whenever I damn well feel like it" or "Men have killed themselves over my beauty and legendary vagina."

Got some ideas? Great.

Now comes the fun part...

The Styles

"Style is a way to say who you are without having to speak."

Rachel Zoe

Chapter 4

Rock & Roll

Do you think when people see Gwen Stefani their first thought is, "Hey, look at that mom." I don't think so. Their first thought probably is, "Hey, look, it's Gwen Stefani. Quick grab my iphone so I can annoy her with a picture." But let's pretend for a second that you didn't know who Gwen Stefani was – *Would you think she looked like a mom?* Of course not. She looks like the coolest woman on the planet. You would be shocked to see her with kids and you would be completely impressed by her boldness, her uniqueness and her total "not-mom-ness". She would inspire you to express yourself… to be you.

If any look says, "I am not a mom" -- it's Rock & Roll. This style has attitude. This style is sexy. This style makes people say, "Who is that bad ass in the school pick up lane?" You want to spice up your marriage? *Rock & Roll.* You want disenfranchised teenagers to stop you on the street and say, "Oh my God, I love your leather mini." *Rock & Roll.* You want to feel your power again? *Rock & Roll.*

Trust me, no other kid is going to mess with your kid at the park when you're dressed in Rock & Roll. Unless they want to feel the sting of a motorcycle boot planted firmly in their pull-ups.

Things you'll need:

1. *Leather jacket* – Go feminine on this one. You want to look cool and sexy, not like you're forming a biker club.

2. *Motorcycle boots* – I'm suggesting motorcycle boots because they're comfortable, but you can wear any black boots you want – pointy ankle boots, stiletto boots, over-the-knee boots. It's all Rock & Roll to me.

3. *Skinny black tie* – Looks great with a vintage rock t-shirt. If you can't find one in a consignment store, try borrowing one from a 1980s comedian.

4. **Black Converse sneakers** – These shoes turn a pair of jeans and t-shirt into an outfit. They're comfortable, they never go out of style and they make you look like you have really great, alternative taste. They're like magic shoes.

5. **Black skinny jeans** - Live in these. Can be shredded or dressy. Just make sure they're tight.

6. **Vintage rock t-shirts** - You can usually find these at thrift stores, but if not, Google "Trunk Ltd". They have amazing, feminine cut rocker tees.

7. **Red skinny jeans** – Fun to wear going out or just about anywhere. Remember: Rock & Roll mamas do not care what people think!

8. **Tiny black mini** – The tinier the better on this one, I'm afraid. Pair with black tights or even fishnets. The great part is that if your tights get torn (which they probably will), it makes the look even cooler.

9. **Metallic tank** – Aim for one that's loose and flowing – Rock & Roll tops don't always have to be tight. (Rock & Roll bottoms do.)

10. **Skull ring** – Doesn't have to be expensive. My kids found a great skull ring for me out of a vending machine.

11. **Tight white t-shirt** -- Scoop neck, spandex blend. Should you wear a black bra under it? Hell, yeah!

12. **Studded belt** – This belt should look like you stole it off your rock star boyfriend while he was passed out.

13. **Black leather chain purse** – Large enough to carry sippy cups and snacks, but cool enough that it looks like you're just carrying drugs and condoms.

A week of outfits:

1. Black skinny jeans, vintage Blondie concert t-shirt, skinny black tie, Converse sneakers.

2. Tiny black mini, fishnets, scoop neck white t-shirt, boots, leather jacket.

3. Red skinny jeans, metallic tank, boots, skull ring.

4. Black skinny jeans, studded belt, white t-shirt, boots, black leather chain purse.

5. Red skinny jeans, vintage Clash t-shirt, studded belt, Converse sneakers, leather jacket.

6. Tiny black mini, studded belt over metallic tank, boots.

7. Red skinny jeans, white t-shirt, studded belt, black Converse sneakers, skull ring.

(Throw in a frayed silvery scarf, a package of temporary tattoos and some heavy black eyeliner and you've not only got a new look, but a completely terrifying transformation.)

Blog Posts

Rock & Roll -- Day 6

"How to get sketchy people to like you"

I love the skate park. On a sunny day there's nothing more fun than watching my children hurl themselves down steep concrete slopes barely clinging to the wheeled objects below them. But there's another element that adds a touch of danger to our skate park outings – the sketchy people that gather there. Sometimes they're happy and drunk by eight a.m., sometimes they're having hillbilly-style shouting matches with each other and sometimes they're just piled closely together in the sun, like a bunch of bored cats.

They never talk to me. I never talk to them. I used to smile at them, but stopped since no smile was ever returned. Sure, we're at the same skate park, but we're in different universes.

That all changed today.

I noticed one of the sketchy people looking at me, then out of the blue he spoke, apologizing for his pit bull being off leash. I told him that I loved dogs and then apologized for my children rolling Cheerios into the largest skate bowl. And just like that, a conversation was afoot. We whiled away the morning talking about tattoos, legalizing marijuana and the ever rising cost of Red Bull. I made some herbal recommendations for his girl-friend's hacking cough while their pit bull dragged my children around by the pants. So what made my sketchy compadre talk to me today? I was the same person I'd always been. *Only my clothes were different.*

It was the first day I'd worn Rock & Roll to the skate park. The change in my style gave this stranger the unconscious signal that I was okay to talk to, whereas my previous mom uniform had told him to stay away. Our clothes are the first clues in people determining who we are. Sloppy or neat, tight or loose, colorful or black, each piece of clothing is a piece of our personality puzzle. And let's face it, our society doesn't really consider moms to be the most exciting group on the planet – as in, "Hey, now the party can really get started – a bunch of moms just showed up!" Maybe that's because our clothes give the information that we're not all that interesting even before we've had a chance to open our mouths.

I can't wait for my husband to meet my new, scary friends!

Rock & Roll -- Day 10

"Finally, jewelry your kids can't break"

Two out of three of my kids are boys -- boys who like to throw things, knock things over and break things all in the name of science. So from very early on, my boys have yearned for an answer to one perplexing question -- How hard does one need to pull on mommy's jewelry before it breaks? Babies and toddlers terrorize jewelry to the point that most moms just stop wearing it. It's one of the first nails in our fashion coffins. By the time they grow out of this phase, we've gotten out of the habit of putting on jewelry and the only thing that will ever hang on our necks again is a pair of bifocals with a whimsical rainbow chord.

Well, I've finally found jewelry that is child proof -- and it's all Rock & Roll. Rock & Roll jewelry is sturdy and chunky. Sometimes it's leather and sometimes it's studded and most of the time it's pretty cheap. I got this necklace for five dollars at a thrift store and my son, August, is more than happy to demonstrate its durability.

Here's the necklace...

Here's August biting the necklace...

And here's August trying really hard to pull the necklace off...

So today the jewelry discovery more than made up for the fact that my Rock & Roll clothes were once again way too tight for my mental and physical comfort level and I was wearing white studded boots and not headed to a rodeo...

Maybe Rock & Roll style has more to offer moms than I thought...

Rock & Roll -- Day 12

"A recipe for Rock & Roll"

I believe there are two types of women in the world. Women who use Halloween as an opportunity to dress like a prostitute and women who don't. And you never know who these women are until you run into them at a Halloween party. They could be doctors, lawyers, city council members – mild-mannered, upstanding citizens suddenly prancing around as French maids, braless cowgirls or everyone's favorite "slutty witch." I fall into the *other* category of women. This year for Halloween I went as an M&M. A costume neither sexy or hip, but it did allow me to eat as much candy as my kids would let me steal from their bags without having to worry that my stomach was sticking out. Could a naughty nurse gorge herself like I did? I think not.

My feelings for mom clothes are the same. If I could go around dressed in a bell diver's suit, I would. Breathable? No. Flaw covering? Extremely. It seems like the biggest issue I'm having with Rock & Roll style is that EVERYTHING IS SO TIGHT! Tight makes me feel conspicuous and conspicuous makes me feel self-conscious and that's the opposite of the goal of this experiment – to find a look I feel great in.

Fortunately, I put together a Rock & Roll outfit I love and I think anyone can wear.

The recipe is simple:

One stretchy white t-shirt – Needs to have a little spandex, scoop neck is nice and it shouldn't come in a pack of three with "Fruit of the Loom" written on it. I got mine at H&M for $12.00.

One pair of dark cigarette jeans – I'm sorry to break this to you, but they do need to be tight. Really tight, even with the word "stretch" on the label. I got mine at a consignment shop for $10.00.

One pair of over-the-knee black boots – Heel or no heel (I chose no heel so I could run around in them) and pick leather over suede for durability. I found mine at a thrift store for $30.00.

One military-style jacket – This is the secret ingredient in this recipe because of its covering capabilities. These jackets are chic, stylish and long enough to cover your butt. I found mine on Overstock.com for $66.00, but I've also seen them on eBay, at thrift stores and of course, military supply stores.

One studded belt – Black and chunky with studs. I found mine at a thrift store for $7.00

Mix all ingredients together and stir up your life.

Rock & Roll -- Day 18

"Inappropriately dressed while holding vegetables"

I hated the clothes I wore yesterday. It wasn't that they looked terrible. They weren't stained. They weren't itchy. But they weren't *me*.

I am not a sleeveless arm person. I am not a tight clothing person. I don't enjoy sucking in my stomach all day to avoid a publicly humiliating muffin-topping experience. And seriously, who goes to pick up produce dressed like they're in a Pat Benatar tribute band? At first I told myself that I was wearing something I hated just because of my fashion quest. It's all part of the experiment, right? But that's not the *whole* truth.

All my life I've often worn clothes I hated. I hated my wedding dress, but I bought it because the salespeople insisted that it looked fantastic on me. I wore a jumpsuit to a college party because another friend was wearing a jumpsuit and promised we'd be the coolest people there and not just two nerds that looked like they just graduated from flight school. When I was seven, I wore my favorite Snoopy dress to a friend's house to impress her, but fell off her roof instead, ripping the dress and only really impressing on her the fact that I lacked good balance.

I've ignored my "don't wear that" inner voice for years and it got me thinking, *"As women, who are we dressing for?"* Some of us dress for men's attention. Some of us dress for other women's approval. And some of us – the very few lucky ones -- dress for ourselves. These women leave the house happy and confident and the rest of us take note. Not that these women care, of course, because they're not dressing for us and that makes us love them even more.

So that's the real fashion goal. To have the knowledge and confidence to just throw together an amazing outfit that I love AND the whole world loves but I DON'T CARE THAT THEY LOVE.

My other goal is to never jump off a roof to impress anyone again.

Even if your dress has Woodstock on it, that doesn't mean you can fly.

Rock & Roll -- Day 31

"The end of Rock & Roll"

The month of January is gone and so are all pretenses I've ever had of the notion I could be cool if I only *dressed* cool. With a mixture of pride and shame, I will now share my discoveries.

Ten things I've learned about Rock & Roll Style...

10. Giant Stevie Nicks-like bell sleeves should not be worn while using a gas stove.

9. It's a slippery slope between rock fashion and pirate fashion --- just ask Johnny Depp.

8. Wearing Rock & Roll clothes does not make listening to "Elmo Sings the ABCs" any easier.

7. Black wool military coats are more effective at picking up pet hair than lint rollers.

6. If you want the weird dad at the park to talk to you, wear a black mini skirt.

5. Faux leather pants really put zing into any clothesline.

4. Children can render a powerful wedgie if you're wearing thong underwear.

3. Skinny jeans get more comfortable once you've had them on a while and lost all circulation in your legs.

2. Crazy high heels should only be worn while sitting.

1. Children will not listen to any adult wearing cheetah pants.

Chapter 5

Euro

Thomas Fuller said, "Good clothes open all doors" and never has that statement been truer than with Euro. This is, obviously, a European style. Think Paris. Think late night candlelit dinners. Think of yourself draped in silk strolling back to your penthouse with your billionaire European businessman boyfriend. Does that sound absolutely nothing like your life? I know. It's not my life either. But when you're wearing Euro, sometimes you get the feeling that it is your life.

When I dressed in Euro, the whole world treated me like royalty. I intimidated people like crazy. It was awesome. Strangers opened doors for me. I was ushered to the front of lines. And the funny thing is, when you're treated with respect something amazing happens – you start to treat yourself with respect. You hold your head up a little higher. You don't just walk – you stride – and you start to radiate an energy that says, "I am somebody." Which by the way, you are. Euro just helps remind you of that.

A word of caution though -- Euro should not be attempted by anyone with children under the age of five. And if you have a baby, you shouldn't be *within a mile* of anyone dressed in Euro. This is not an "I can just Oxyclean it" style.

Things you'll need:

(Just because Euro looks like an expensive style, doesn't mean it has to be an expensive style. If you can't find everything you're looking for at a consignment shop, check out the sale racks at department stores or go hunting at Ross, T.J. Maxx and Marshalls.)

1. ***Silk button-down shirt*** – Go for a rich color – burgundy, cream or a dark grey.

2. ***Silky lingerie top*** – Looks amazing under a cashmere cardigan or tuxedo jacket.

3. ***Cashmere cardigan*** – Drape it over your shoulders or wear it with a scarf -- just don't get it in a loud color. Euros never wear colors like "kelly green" or "bubblegum pink".

4. ***Tuxedo jacket*** – The goal is to not look like a waiter here, so find a tuxedo jacket that's small and fitted.

5. ***Chic, sparkly tank*** – Rotate this tank with the lingerie top and you've got a ton of outfits.

6. ***Elegant black pants*** -- Wide leg, creased, with pockets. These are grown up pants, people.

7. ***Pencil skirt*** – Pencil skirts can be found in a bunch of different styles. For Euro, look for one that is red, cream or black with a slit in the back.

8. ***Deep red winter coat*** – I found mine at the Burlington Coat Factory for next to nothing and it took my Euro look up to a whole new level. I started to feel like a foreign diplomat.

9. ***Elegant white pants*** – My kids are young enough that it even scares me to write the words "white pants". But if you can wear them without getting them filthy in five seconds, go for it. It's a Euro must.

10. ***Lux weekender bag*** – A Louis Vuitton knock off would work here or any big, leather purse, as long as it's not tacky. Avoid a purse with a ton of zippers. I don't care how expensive they are -- they look cheap.

11. ***Black ankle boots*** – Elegant and simple. Pointy heel.

12. ***Skinny chic belt*** - Gold or silver detail.

13. ***Low slingbacks*** – Black, black, black.

14. ***Big silk scarf*** – Get a richly patterned scarf and drape it over everything from a cardigan to a silk button-down to a tuxedo jacket.

15. ***Jackie O sunglasses*** - Bigger is better. It's not grandma -- it's glam!

16. ***Ballet flats*** – Cheetah or snakeskin. Euros do love to wear dead animals

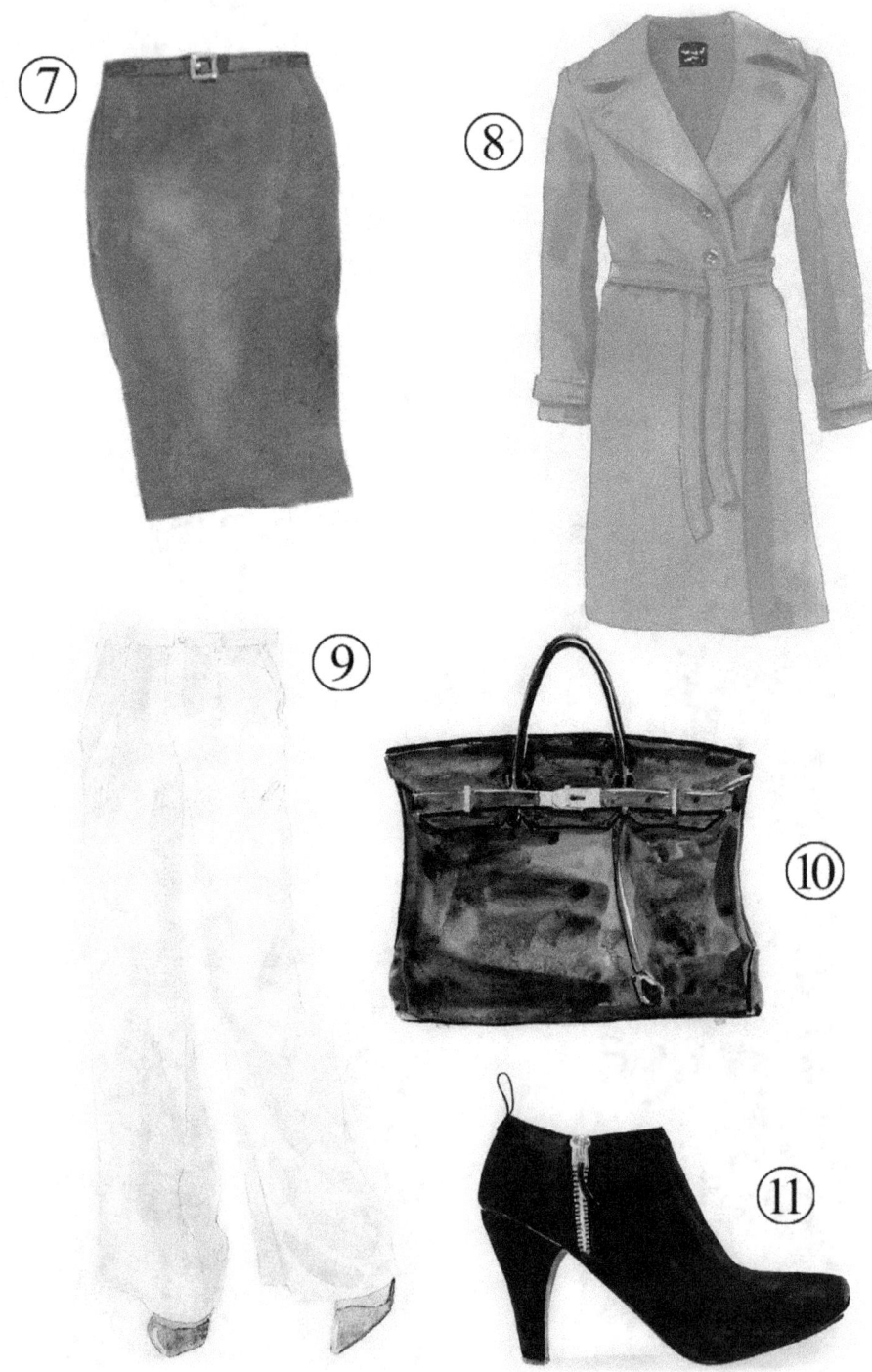

⑫

⑬

⑭

⑮

⑯

A week of outfits:

1. Cream-colored button-down shirt, black pants, deep red winter coat, black ankle boots, skinny chic belt, Jackie O sunglasses. (For warmer weather, replace the red coat with a big scarf.)

2. Chic sparkly tank, tuxedo jacket, elegant white pants, low slingbacks, lux weekend bag.

3. Silky lingerie top, pencil skirt, cashmere cardigan, low slingbacks.

4. Burgundy silk button-down, elegant white pants, skinny chic belt, ballet flats, big scarf, Jackie O sunglasses.

5. Silky lingerie top, black pants, skinny chic belt, pointy boots, Jackie O sunglasses.

6. Deep grey silky button-down, black pants, black ankle boots, big scarf, skinny chic belt.

7. Burgundy silk button-down, pencil skirt, skinny chic belt, low slingbacks, big scarf.

Blog Posts

Euro -- Day 3

"Even the cigar shows respect"

I went to Starbucks yesterday. Nothing unusual about that at all – I try to keep an equal blood to caffeine ratio in my veins at all times. And it's the same Starbucks I always go to with the same characters I see every day. The only difference was that I was wearing Euro.

As I approached the door, I saw someone from inside rushing towards me. I looked up and this man, a complete stranger, had broken out of his hard-earned place in line to *open the door for me*. I was so startled at first that I assumed he knew me, but I had never seen him before. I mumbled "Thank you" and then he said, "Are you in a hurry? Would you like my place in line?"

I'm not joking. This actually happened. When does that ever happen at Starbucks? Actually, when does that happen anywhere? It's like a story I'd tell my kids, *In the olden days, legend has it that men used to open doors for women. They'd even have these special hats they would "tip" as a sign of respect.* I became so flustered that instead of taking the man up on his kind line-butting offer, I did the mature thing and hid in the bathroom until he left.

I chalked the experience up to just a strange anomaly until later that day when my family and I went to a museum. I was standing in line, at least five people deep, when the woman behind the counter shouted, "Ma'am, can I help you?" Confused, I turned around to see who she was talking to. Had Hilary Clinton just arrived? The woman gestured towards me again, smiled and repeated her question, even shooing the people in front of me out of *my way*.

And why? I've been to Starbucks and the museum a zillion times and I've always been treated the same way – like just another grating member of the disheveled mom club. But not today. Today I was special because today I was wearing "important people clothing." Two thoughts ran through my head. The first was the sad realization that human beings must be the most warped creatures to have ever roamed the Earth.

Our judgments are so quick and baseless, created solely on appearance, what hope is there of ever having a united and peaceful planet? My second thought was, I LOVE EURO!

Euro -- Day 4

"I'm already Euro cracking"

It's a mere four days into my month of Euro and I have *completely run out of clothes.* They all had to be dropped off at the dry cleaners yesterday and I won't be getting them back for several days. I cobbled together the remaining items in my closet in an attempt to look Euro, but ending up looking (and feeling) more like a cranky German tourist.

It appears that wearing Euro style is going to need more forethought. I can't just throw something in the wash for the next day. I'm going to need a word that's not really in my vocabulary -- a word called *planning.* I am not a planner. Oh sure, I plan on being a planner... someday. I have a dream of a big, organized calendar on the wall with our lives laid out before us in whimsical handwriting. Things will be written on it like, *Dentist tomorrow! Grandma arrives! Cat neutering – brace yourself, Rusty!* (This would be accompanied by a little frowny face sticker). But alas, that calendar does not exist yet and somehow I find myself every night standing in my kitchen thinking, *I should have planned a meal.* Why does dinner always seem to sneak up on me?

So I thought I'd take some clothes planning advice from the icon of Euro style, Catherine Deneuve. She is a very famous French actress and has been the absolute epitome of this look every day for pretty much her entire life. But since I don't actually know Catherine Deneuve, I'm just going to have to make up our conversation in the hopes of finding inspiration in what I *think* she might say.

Me: *Hi, Ms. Deneuve, thanks so much for sitting down with me today.*

Catherine Deneuve: *I am not sitting down with you today. You are making this entire conversation up. I am somewhere fabulous while you are alone talking to yourself. If you had better health care in America, I would suggest you seek it.*

Me: *What I'm seeking is your advice on clothes. How far in advance do you plan your wardrobe?*

Catherine Deneuve: *I do not plan it at all. I am an artist. I need to feel inspiration in all things before I begin them and my clothes are no exception.*

Me: *But if you had to "ball park it" are we talking like a day in advance? A week in advance?*

Catherine Deneuve: *You and I are not talking right now. We have established this. And I don't know what a ballpark is.*

Me: *Look, I need your help. I'm a mom with three kids and I'm trying to look fabulously Euro all month. How do you keep your clothes so clean without having an astronomical dry cleaning bill?*

Catherine Deneuve: *By never, ever getting them dirty.*

Me: *But what if you're making chocolate-dipped Rice Krispy treats with your kids? What if you need to open the chicken coop and it's raining? What if you win free tickets to a monster truck rally?*

Catherine Deneuve: *I would not do any of those things. Euro is all about silk, cashmere and crocodile heels – the finest of materials. This is the utmost consideration in your daily life.*

Me: *Wait, you wear shoes made from actual crocodiles? I find that so sad.*

Catherine Deneuve: *What I find sad is that you give your children chocolate-encrusted hardened cereal as a dessert, stomp around in the rain with livestock and go watch ridiculously oversized American vehicles smash into each other and consider it entertainment.*

...At this point, Catherine Deneuve angrily stomps out of my mind. As with all things, this was not *planned*...

Euro -- Day 17

"The Euro endurance outfit"

I actually *liked* the outfit I wore yesterday, so much so that I didn't immediately tear it off as soon as I got home to put on my "eatin' pants". I have several pairs of "eatin' pants", but they all have the same wonderful quality -- you can eat as much as you want in them and thanks to their stretchy or drawstring waistbands, you can never, ever feel fat. They are worn during all major candy holidays where I can easily work my way through several large chocolate bunnies (we're talking solid, not hollow), a generous-sized Christmas stocking or someone's unattended Halloween bag without so much as the slightest feeling of tightness around my waist that screams *stop eating, you disgusting pig*. They are on the short-list of things I would save if our house ever caught on fire... children, animals, eatin' pants. But my treasured pants actually stayed in the closet in favor of my Euro outfit.

I went to the flea market in it. I made playdough in it. I pushed a wheelbarrow of firewood in it, threw the ball for our dog in it, played trucks on the floor in it and went to a friend's house for dinner in it. The ballet flats hurt after a while, but most Euro shoes hurt *in the box before you put them on*, so "after a while" felt like an improvement.

Here are the essentials to this highly recommended outfit –

Jeans -- Notice I didn't put the word "mom" in front of jeans. They should be nice jeans – no pleats or holes and without the bejeweled words, "Hot Bottom" written on the back.

Slightly painful metallic ballet flats

Black silk shirt purchased at a thrift store for ten dollars

Cashmere sweater purchased at a thrift store for twenty dollars

My daughter's cheetah scarf that she wears while playing "angry wild cat that also likes to look pretty and eat squeeze yogurts."

This outfit wasn't so dressy that I intimidated strangers and made them grovel at my feet (a plus or minus depending on how you look at it). It might not even be the Euro outfit I have looked best in so far, but here's the thing - *I felt my best in it.* And that's the goal, isn't it? I felt comfortable and more importantly, I felt like me. *Me in Euro.* And that is worth the "f" word. That is truly *fabulous.*

Euro -- Day 24

"I've never been more dressed up to buy powdered sugar"

      Normally, on a Sunday morning, if I had to run to the grocery store to buy just one thing, I'd remain in my pajamas to do so. But those days are long gone. I had to make cookies for my daughter's Brownie troop and we were missing powdered sugar. I quickly looked through my closet and assessed that I had absolutely nothing clean to wear except a pair of black silk pants, a burgundy top, a plaid jacket and three inch heels. So that is what I wore… to buy powdered sugar… at nine o'clock on a Sunday morning… at the grocery store…

      And I actually felt good about it. I know the powdered sugar appreciated it and although most of the shoppers remained immersed in their own slow pursuits of Velveeta and Buffalo wings, some definitely gave me the look. You know the look I'm talking about – the one that says either, "You go girl" or "You go girl *straight to the nearest mental health facility*", depending on how you want to interpret their interpretation of my outfit.

      Either way, I felt a world of possibilities open up to me. After all, I'm always running to the grocery store for some forgotten item and shopping is simply more fun dressed in inappropriately fancy clothes. What will I wear to buy butter? Basmati rice deserves a themed outfit. And, of course, I can't wait to rock the dog food aisle…

Euro -- Day 28

"Are you going somewhere?"

That is the question I have most often received during the month of Euro. *Are you going somewhere?* People take one look at how dressed up I am at whatever non-dressy place I am and quickly assume this must not be my last stop. *Surely, after the park, she's off to cocktails with the President...*

Euro is a powerful look. It demands respect by way of silk, cashmere and super pointy heels. Wearers of this look beware – you will not go unnoticed. You will be treated as *better*. You will no longer just walk into a room -- you will *sweep* into it. And no matter where you go in this look, you will be thought of as *the person in charge*.

This look was so healing for me because no one treats moms with any respect. We're just these lumpy, stain-covered beings with little crying creatures hanging on us. Most of the time we're ignored and if we're not ignored, we're criticized. *Your baby needs a hat.* How many of us have heard that one from a stranger? No "hello". No "You're doing a great job." No "I'll watch your kids if you'd like a nap." Just, "Let me point out something you don't need to hear right now."

I've always assumed moms were treated this way because our society just doesn't value the job we're doing. But that is only *part* of the problem. The other part lies within us. I don't treat myself with respect so why should anyone else? I skip meals or just eat whatever is left over and half-eaten on my kid's plates. I barely shower and dress like I permanently have the flu and I never, ever take time for myself to do something as simple as go on a walk or even read a magazine.

I ignore myself, so society is just taking a cue from me. I know this is true because the *Euro mom is never ignored.* By simply changing my clothes, I not only changed the way I was treated by the world, but I changed the way I treated myself. If I can take the time to look decent, I can also take the time to eat. And sit. And breathe… What a positively *European* concept.

So when someone says to me, "Are you going somewhere?" I say this: *Yes, I'm going everywhere. I'm here.*

A Word About Shoes...

      I have specifically chosen to not include a bunch of shoes in my style suggestions. With a few exceptions, I've tried to limit it to just a few pairs for each style. Why? Because shoes are expensive and this book is intended to help you find your style, not put you in a debtor's prison. I've tried to select shoes that are cute, comfortable and mom friendly (except in the cases of Euro and Bombshell), so that you can get a feel for the style without breaking your bank account. Once you've discovered your style, by all means, let your shoe addiction get dangerously out of control. I know mine is. We can form a support group together and have weekly meetings at different shoe stores.

Chapter 6

Slacker Mom

Okay, remember the great way you were treated in Euro? Well, you can totally forget about it with Slacker. No one is going to open any doors for you when you're a Slacker Mom. But because you're a Slacker Mom, you won't really care. Screw them, right? Uptight losers.

The great thing about Slacker is that most moms already dress in a kind of slacker way, so the look isn't that big of a departure. The key is to turn what you've already got *into a style*. This means balancing the big and comfortable with the cool, feminine and sexy.

Regular mom uniform - Pleated jeans, oversized Old Navy t-shirt, big white sneakers and baseball hat.

Slacker Mom uniform -- *Skinny* Jeans, *flannel plaid* shirt, *flip-flops* and *trucker* hat.

Not that big of a change, right? Fortunately, sometimes it's the subtle changes that make the biggest difference. Slacker takes years, I'm talking *years*, off the dowdy mom look. And who knows? Maybe you'll even trade in that minivan for a skateboard and start growing the best weed ever in one of your Home Depot flower boxes. And when your family and friends confront you with an intervention, you'll just roll your eyes and say, *Whatever...*

Things you'll need:

1. *Awesome bad attitude t-shirts* -- Remind the world how little you care with cute, feminine cut t-shirts. Some of my favorites are, "It just doesn't matter", "It's not me, it's you" and "Since when did that become my problem?"

2. *Frayed jeans mini skirt* – Choose any above-the-knee length you like as long as it's frayed and worn looking.

3. **Vintage flannel shirt** – Thrift stores always have a butt load of flannels. Can be mens or womens. Wear it as a shirt or tie it around your waist for an essential Slacker accessory. (It's a great trick when wearing a frayed jeans mini and you'd like to hide the cellulite monster that lives on the back of your legs.)

4. **Faded torn jeans** – Go for skinny on these. This style can look bulky if you're not careful.

5. **Cargo pants** – Can be rolled or cropped.

6. **Trucker hat** – Looks cute with everything.

7. **Sexy lingerie top** – This might just be the most important item in the Slacker look because it's a counter-weight to all the sloppiness. I suggest getting a couple lingerie tops and several spaghetti strap tanks in a variety of colors and rotate them. It's a great way to expand your wardrobe inexpensively.

8. **Work boots** – Get ready to start clomping around.

9. **Flip-flops** – Yes, flip-flops. And a pedicure.

10. **Chic sweat pants** - Classic grey is great as long as they are chic and don't say, "Russell" or "Champion" anywhere on them.

11. **Gold stackable rings** – Delicate jewelry is key to balancing this look.

12. **Ethnic fair trade messenger bag** – So Portland! So Slacktivist! So "I sort of care about the environment."

13. **Vintage army jacket** – Military supply stores have the best.

A week of outfits:

1. Cute tank top, chic sweatpants, flip-flops, trucker hat.

2. Bad attitude t-shirt, cropped cargo pants, work boots, delicate jewelry.

3. Sexy lingerie top, vintage flannel shirt tied around your waist, shredded skinny jeans, work boots.

4. Frayed jeans mini skirt, bad attitude t-shirt, flip-flops.

5. Cargo pants, cute tank top, flip-flops.

6. Chic sweatpants, sexy lingerie top, vintage flannel shirt buttoned halfway, work boots.

7. Frayed jeans mini skirt, tank top, vintage flannel tied around your waist, flip-flops.

Blog Posts

(Note: I did not try out Slacker Mom during **My Year of Fabulous***, so I don't have blog posts for this one. Just for fun, I've included a random blog post for some body image inspiration.)*

"Ten awesome things about a mom body"

I have a mom body. It makes sense, right? Football players have football player bodies, ballet dancers have ballet dancer bodies and moms have *mom bodies.* We each have own our specialty and in my opinion, creating life kind of trumps catching a ball for a touchdown or twirling in the air with an eating disorder. So why is the mom body held in such disdain? Why is it that 64% of women feel worse about their bodies after they become moms? Can you imagine an ultimate fighter leaving the ring and saying, "Don't look at my nose! It's so swollen!" And having a baby is a lot like being an ultimate fighter except our fight lasts nine months without so much as a water break or a Nike endorsement.

Well, I'm sick of society trash-talking my junk. I think our culture doesn't celebrate the mom body because very few people actually know all the things it can do. After all, in order to love Superman, it helps to know he can fly. That's why I've compiled a list of all the amazing things a mom body is capable of – an official scorecard of our secret super powers. It's time for the world to stand back and be awed by us for a change. It's time to look at the mom body in *a whole new way.*

1. Mom Boobs. Perky boobs can only do one thing – look perky. But mom boobs can do a *variety* of things. These long thin bad boys have give. They have reach. Mom boobs can be used as an impromptu scarf, a slim jim for unlocking car doors or as fun, irreverent cat toys. Mom boobs can even improve your sex life. You and your significant other can go at it and you don't even have to be in the same room. Just roll one of them out of your bra, send it cascading out the door and watch the sparks fly.

2. The Bellybutton. Sure, most people can wink with their eyes, but really, how boring is that? My eyes AND my belly button can wink and since my belly button is always in a half-closed winking position, it's like I'm constantly flirting with the world. Like right now, I'm winking at you, through my shirt. My belly button has turned into one subtle, protruding piece of flesh and I'm happy to add it to my alluring female bag of tricks.

3. The Pooch. Talk about perky! Big and round like Pooh Bear, the mom tummy puffs proudly out of any pair of jeans saying to the world, "Never forget I've had a baby!" The mom pooch is a great place to rest your hands. It's a great place to eat off of. I recently planted an herb garden on my mom pooch. Just don't make the mistake of trying to tame your tummy underneath a pair of Spanx. The mom pooch is a most vengeful body part and will seek justice by exploding out of the top or bottom of whatever restraining device you're trying to suppress it with. Which is fine by me. I say, the bigger the better. No gut, no glory!

4. The Vagina. Remember when you were a kid and you'd laugh so hard you'd pee in your pants? Well, the mom vagina helps you recreate this magical experience on a daily basis. And not just with laughing. A small sneeze, a startle or a delayed trip to the bathroom and suddenly you're relieving yourself whenever and wherever you want. And talk about size! Your super-sized snatch provides you with no more pain at the gynecologist, no more fear of extra large tampons and no more wondering where to keep extra Christmas decorations. Thanks, big vagina! I haven't had to buy storage containers for years.

5. Cartoon Feet. Most moms have feet Fred Flintstone would kill for. Feet can grow a lot in pregnancy and mine are now approximately the size of two loaves of sourdough bread. I love padding around on my two puffy, calloused clouds and love even more that my children can use them as floaties at the beach.

6. Awesome Rounded Shoulders. Moms carry babies around so much that our shoulders are permanently rounded. Rounded shoulders make it so much easier to get through doors and can eventually lead to a hump – and everyone knows humps are good luck.

7. A really weird butthole. My friend confessed the other day that she could no longer wear thong underwear because she has permanent hemorrhoids after giving birth. Well, great because who wants to wear thong underwear anyway? Thong underwear only looks good on like five people and for the rest of us, it turns our butts into a display case for cellulite. Now you have a medical reason to avoid these evil contraptions and enter the far more comfortable world of mom underwear – cotton briefs so big they could double as a picnic blanket or an all-weather car cover.

8. Gigantic man arms. Oh sure, the rest of our bodies might be gelatinous heaps of goo, but thanks to holding another human being 12 hours a day for years on end, our arms are pure redneck truck driver. These massive hunks of man-muscle bulge out of any dainty sweater. Put on a sundress and it's drag queen time.

9. A wide, flat butt. Hey, all you non-moms out there with flat stomachs. We moms have something on our bodies that is flatter than all of your stomachs combined. *And that's our butts.* And we didn't have to go to the gym three times a week to get them. In fact, we didn't have to do anything at all. The large, flat butt serves as your back pocket's best friend. Last year, I put my entire tax return in my back pocket and didn't even bend the edges.

10. The Baby. By far the most impressive feature of the mom body, your baby is proof that your body can form a brain, spinal column, every major organ, eyes, hands and feet all while you're sitting on the couch mindlessly watching QVC. What superhero can do that? So the next time you hear a awful comment about the mom body or you look in the mirror and wonder what happened to your former self, stand tall, be proud and know that this awesome and *very changed* thing you walk around in every day can create miracles.

Chapter 7

Classic

Muffy, is that you? I can't believe it! I thought you died in the 80's when the Ralph Lauren factory exploded. But you're still here and I've got to say, you are a great style for so many moms.

Classic style is East Coast, waspy perfection – a simple white oxford, crisp khaki pants and long, silky hair held back in an effortless ponytail. (Normally, I'm against the mom ponytail, but I highly encourage it when it comes to Classic.) Think Charlotte from "Sex and the City". Think horsey girl with great skin and amazingly white teeth. Think county club that only lets in *certain* kinds of people.

When you wear Classic Style, you instantly feel more organized. Sure, your house has piles of laundry as far as the eye can see and your children are running around naked and covered in glitter glue, but everyone will assume you've got it all under control because you're dressed in Classic. Other moms will enviously imagine that you're home at night baking cookies and scrapbooking your latest trip to Costa Rica while lounging in a cable knit sweater and drinking a glass of chardonnay.

Okay, you're not. I'm not. That mom is an urban myth. But thanks to Classic, that urban myth will forever be alive and well. This style works for any mom with kids of any age, but one note of caution -- Classic *looks* easy, but it's simplicity actually makes it a trickier style to pull off. Put the wrong khaki pants and white shirt together and instead of embodying understated perfection, you'll look like a park ranger.

Things you'll need:

1. *Jeans jacket* – Can be worn with anything from a turtleneck to pearls. Just don't wear it with jeans unless you want to look like you work at a rodeo.

2. *Short, fitted blazer* – Go for tan. It's preppy adorable and dresses up any outfit.

3. *Turtleneck sweater* – Not too bulky. Black, navy or grey works great.

4. *Khaki pants* – Flat front, ankle length, skinny or cropped. Avoid pleated. Pleated khaki pants just say "male math teacher."

5. *Short-sleeved polo shirt* – Get a wide variety of colors. Vintage Izod shirts with the alligator on are fun to wear.

6. *White button-down shirt* – The essential Classic item. Can be lived in.

7. *Plaid doctor's bag* – Putting a little plaid in your Classic look is so old school L.L. Bean. Carrying around a doctor's bag is functional and cool.

8. *Straight leg jeans* – Not skinny, but fitted.

9. *Equestrian boots* -- These shouldn't look like you've actually just jumped off a horse, but more "equestrian boot inspired".

10. *Ballet flats* – Can have a bow or buckle.

11. *Jack Purcells* – I think wearing white sneakers is the biggest fashion mistake anyone can make EXCEPT in this case. Jack Purcells have a great vintage vibe and they are so East-Coast-summer-at-the-tennis-club awesome.

12. *Pearl necklace* – Hardly anyone on Earth can tell the difference between real pearls and fake pearls, so save your money and go for fake.

13. *A-line skirt* – Corduroy A-line for winter, linen A-line for summer.

14. *Summer dress* – Classics wear a lot of dresses. To lunch with friends. To Mommy and me class. To walk to the mailbox. It doesn't really matter the destination. The point is to look put together.

15. *Skinny brown leather belt* – Goes with everything. Find a nice one because you'll wear it a lot.

A week of outfits:

1. White button-down shirt, straight leg jeans, ballet flats, skinny brown leather belt, pearls.

2. Khaki pants, skinny brown leather belt, equestrian boots, turtleneck sweater, plaid doctor's bag.

3. Summer dress, ballet flats, pearls.

4. Straight leg jeans, Jack Purcells, short-sleeved polo shirt.

5. A-line skirt, white button-down shirt, jeans jacket, ballet flats.

6. Turtleneck sweater, tan blazer, straight leg jeans, equestrian boots.

7. A-line skirt, short-sleeved polo, Jack Purcells.

(In warmer weather, replace turtleneck with either polo shirt or white button-down.)

Blog Posts

Classic -- Day 1

"Perfection is in the air this May"

Raised on the East Coast by my Mummy and Daddy (but mostly by nannies), I am well-bred, well-educated and well-refined. I am never late. I am always organized. My kids are stain-free and polite. They speak Mandarin Chinese. I taught them myself. I am never without my horse, my charity and my opinions. I do Pilates. I read the Wall Street Journal. My show-stopping children's birthday parties will make your kid's party look like a prison barbecue. I am redecorating our house for the third time. I am never frazzled. My sheer existence will make you question *everything you hold dear about yourself.*

Oh sure, I have a hidden drinking problem, but you'll never know it because I can afford to go to the most discreet and luxurious rehab facilities. I will come back from these "spa trips" tan, rested and more committed to perfection than ever. And if you're a normal mom and our kids are in the same class and you happen to have the misfortune of signing up for a committee that I'm in charge of… *I will be your worst nightmare.*

I am… Classic.

Classic -- Day 7

"The first rule of the outlet mall"

1) *The first rule of the outlet mall: Do not talk about the outlet mall.*

2) *Second rule of the outlet mall: Do not talk about the outlet mall.*

3) *Third rule of the outlet mall: Do not talk about the outlet mall.*

And why? Because if you talked about the outlet mall you'd start to realize that it is not *really cheaper than the regular mall.* Oh, yes, everywhere you look at the outlet mall there are signs screaming that you're saving a bundle, but they're only there to try and desperately hide what we all know is true.

That a maxi dress marked down from ONE HUNDRED AND SIX-TY DOLLARS to ONE HUNDRED DOLLARS is still ONE HUNDRED DOLLARS and therefore, too expensive -- especially if you're a mom and you know there's a good chance the dress is going to get stained. An outlet mall is kind of like walking into a greasy diner with signs that say "fat free cheeseburgers". All the customers look around, wink at each other and make a silent denial agreement… *let's just go with it.*

And go with it, I did. I raked in the Classic clothes and not a moment too soon. Yesterday, I left the house like this –

I felt like a "Republican party intern". Then I ran into a friend who told me I looked more like a *lesbian going on a job interview*. (This friend is a lesbian so she knows what she's talking about.) It's not quite the Classic angle I envisioned, but hey, people are talking about my clothes. *Go me!*

So because of the everything-is-on-sale-but-still-very-expensive-outlet-mall, I think I just may have successfully pulled my Classic airplane out of a death spiral. We'll see what you think tomorrow. But, I'm already feeling a bit more perfect.

Classic -- Day 17

"A day in the life of a Classic"

Today I'm having one of those *mom days* that is so full of fabulous, my biggest problem is choosing *what to wear…* Just take a look at my dance card –

Septic service -- I start off the day waiting for the septic guy to empty our tank. Not a lot is required of me for this task except to be nauseated and then sign a check, but still, I want to look my best. The septic guy stares at poop all day, he doesn't also need to stare at me in my Super Bowl half shirt and leggings.

Sick child -- My oldest son is sick so I got a whole chicken to make broth. I really hate handling large, raw chicken and pulling out that creepy mystery bag inside the bird, but I don't want my outfit to reflect my unhappiness. I want to look professional, but still feminine – butcher chic.

Dentist appointment -- My daughter has a dentist appointment. Nothing reminds you that you live the pampered life of a one-percenter like taking one child to the dentist along with your *other child who is sick*. I'm going to get a lot of dirty looks in the waiting room for this so I need to dress for the *spotlight*.

Play date -- My daughter, sick son and I will then pick up their brother from a play date. When my kids haven't seen each other in a while, they usually fight and drive me crazy for at least an hour, so my outfit needs to be cute and casual and ready to separate biting children off the floor.

Kid's Kung Fu in the afternoon – I'm in full chauffeur mode now. I want my outfit to look like I have an interesting life, but in fact I'm just staring at twitter on my phone waiting for the class to be over.

Dinner – Me, three children, chicken soup. *Oh, what to wear… what to wear…*

Clean up -- My husband usually comes home after dinner and I certainly don't want to greet him looking haggard, holding an empty glass of wine and half-heartedly cleaning the kitchen. He's seen that *a thousand times*.

Bath and story time – This outfit is in some ways the most essential outfit of the day. It needs to be chic, yet durable (there's water involved) but most importantly, it needs to be comfortable. I usually fall asleep reading to my kids and I don't want to wake up at three o'clock in the morning wearing a linen sundress. I'm thinking silk pajamas or at the very least, a caftan.

So that's my day. I've decided to go with this outfit –

-- because nothing says "septic" and "soup" like a blazer and pearls. Of course, I might have to make a few costume changes along the way, but hey, that's all part of the fabulous life of being a mom.

Classic -- Day 20

"A Classic makes a style decision"

Have you ever known you were going to break up with someone, but you just had to wait a little bit? Maybe you had planned a great trip together and you still really wanted to go so you think, *I'll just wait until after Cancun to break up with this idiot…* Or maybe you want to wait until after Christmas. Boxing Day is always a nice day to lower the hammer on a soon-to-be-ex. I knew a couple that waited until their children had left for college before *mutually dumping each other.* That not only takes planning, but years of some pretty good acting.

I'm ready to break up with Classic. In my heart I know it's not working out, but I have to wait eleven more days until the end of May. For busy moms, *location is key to style.* We need a style that looks good on us, is inexpensive and very easily accessible. Most moms barely have time to brush their teeth much less hunt in a hundred mile radius looking for the

perfect skirt. I am not in a Classic location like New England, so there aren't any Classic clothes at consignment or thrift shops -- which means the clothes are more expensive and harder to find -- which means they are not for me. Yesterday, as I was walking through our yard in white pants, my son accidentally threw mud my way. As I looked down at my totally trashed, too fussy outfit, all I could think of was, *we are so breaking up.*

A Word About Purses...

Like shoes, it is a common perception to think that you need a lot of purses to survive and it's hard not to get lost in the fantasy that you'll be that woman who has a purse for every occasion. *Did you see the purse Janice took to the gynecologist? How did she find the perfect shade of gunmetal to match the stirrups?*

But in this book I'm suggesting that you just carry one purse per style and it's always a big one. Why? Because moms carry a Sherpa amount of stuff in their purses, so you need something chic, but really roomy. Just don't buy an expensive purse. The mommy purse gets dragged through the mud – literally, sometimes – and clothes should make you happy, not turn you into raging lunatic who screams things like, "Why is there an opened jar of honey in my new Michael Kors bag????"

Chapter 8

Sporty Chic

Hey, you! Yeah, *you* -- sitting on your couch right now reading this book. Do you have a snack nearby? Maybe just an opened jar of Nutella with a spoon resting on your gut? Me, too. Great. We're both hopelessly out of shape. I'm probably a lot more out of shape than you are. My body after children looks like an experimental art installation. I have so many varicose veins on my legs it looks like my knees have dreadlocks. My son uses the stretched out skin on my stomach to hide his matchbox cars. And my breasts? Well, let's just say I use them as a convenient airline pillow.

If you want to be a Sporty Chic mom and the only thing that's holding you back is your body and the fact that you never ever exercise, I'm here to tell you that you can still be Sporty Chic. These days Sporty Chic clothes are much more flattering than ever and you can buy them almost anywhere. You can find a complete Sporty Chic wardrobe at high-end places like Athleta and Lululemon or super stores like Costco, Walmart and Big Five. However, the Sporty Chic wardrobe is not cheap. I don't like shopping second hand for exercise clothes because it makes me feel like I'm buying someone else's crotch sweat. So because I bought everything new, my Sporty Chic wardrobe ended up being the most expensive look in my style trial.

Sporty Chic, out of all the looks, has the most power over the wearer. Put on Sporty Chic and you'll suddenly want to be more active. You'll stretch. You'll try to touch your toes. You might even jog behind the stroller for a block. Your clothes will inspire you to have more fun -- to get out there and do something. And you won't have to make a New Years' resolution or lock your refrigerator or pay for head to toe lipo. It'll just happen.

All you have to do is go shopping.

Things you'll need:

1. *Below-the-knee yoga pants* – Go for black. They're the most forgiving.

2. *Long yoga pants* – Also black. I think a little flared at the bottom makes them look more chic.

3. *Skort* – A skort is a skirt/shorts combination. A spork is a spoon/fork combination. Wear a skort while eating with a spork for a delightful wordplay activity.

4. *Razor-back dress* – I love these dresses. So sporty, so sexy. Mom arms are the most in shape part of our bodies, so why not show them off?

5. *Yoga-inspired long-sleeved t-shirt* – Adds a little Zen zest to your wardrobe. Bonus – gives the illusion that you're spiritually centered.

6. *Cashmere hoodie* – If you can't find one inexpensively, just go for a hoodie that's all one color with a thin, drapey material. You don't want to end up looking like a professional boxer.

7. *Long quilted winter coat* – Incredibly warm, yet fabulous and functional.

8. *Retro sneakers* – Fun, quirky, comfortable. Adds color to the Sporty Chic wardrobe.

9. *Athletic all-purpose sandals* – And I don't mean those Teva sandals with the Velcro straps. Go for brands like Jambu, J-41 or Ahnu.

10. *Adventure khaki pants* – These pants are made of a tougher material and can take whatever your kids dish out. My favorites are Athleta's Dipper pants.

11. *Fitted spaghetti strap tank* – All colors. Wear it under a cashmere hoodie or just by itself.

12. *Sleek backpack* – Go for a solid color and not too bulky.

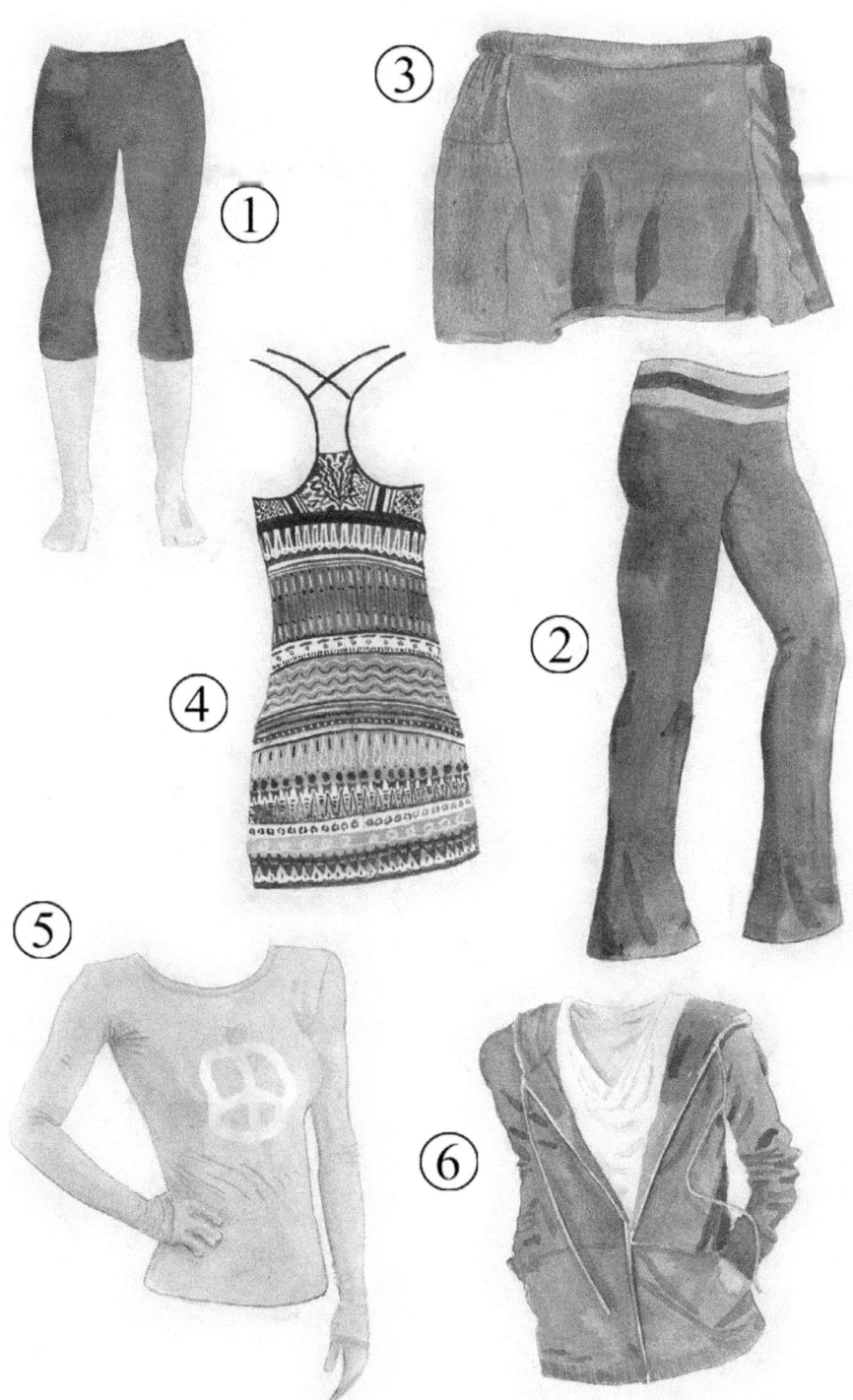

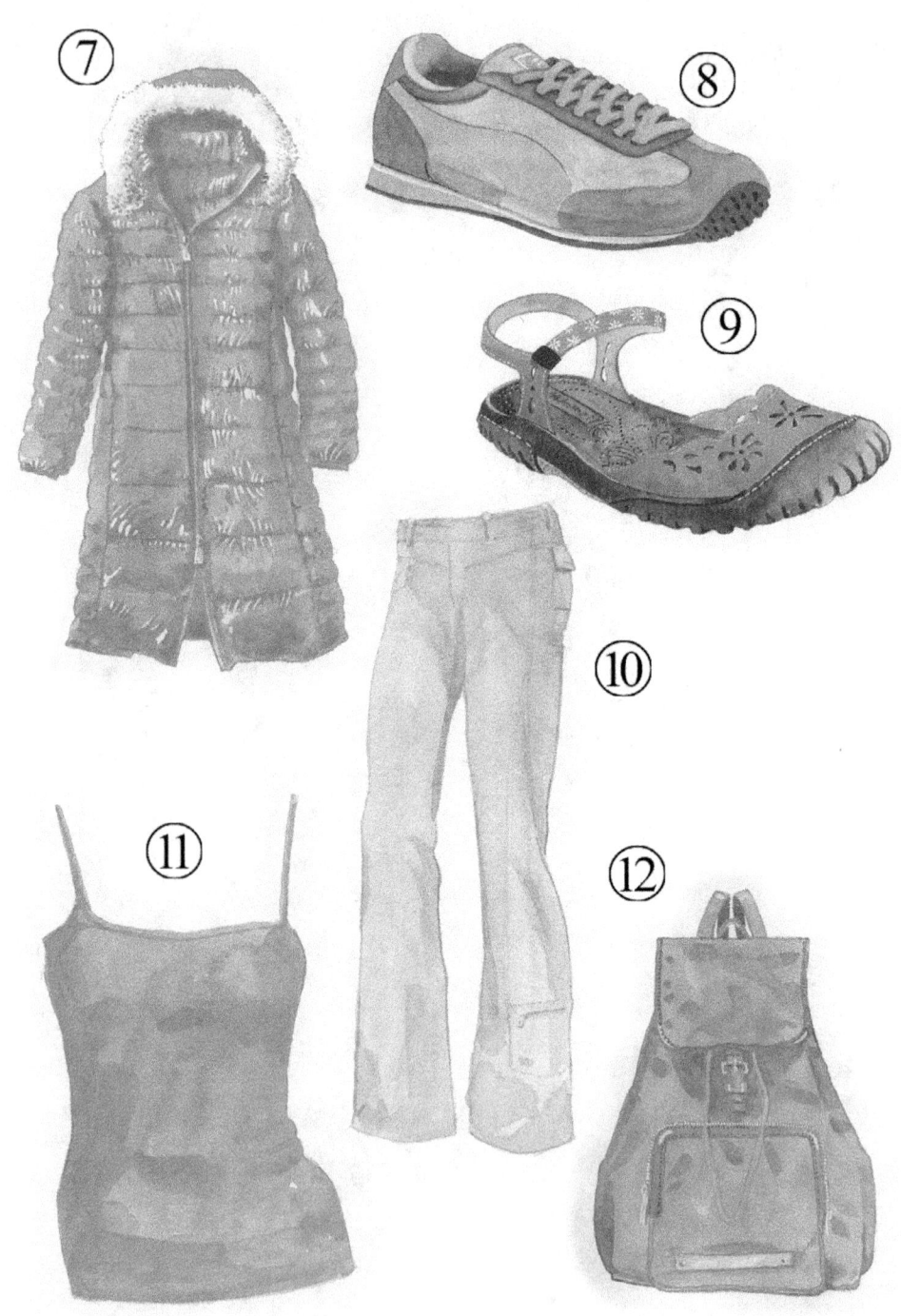

A week of outfits:

1. Adventure khaki pants, tank top, athletic all-purpose sandals.

2. Skort, tank top, cashmere hoodie, retro sneakers.

3. Yoga-inspired long sleeved t-shirt, long yoga pants, athletic all-purpose sandals.

4. Below-the-knee yoga pants, tank top, cashmere hoodie, retro sneakers.

5. Razor-back dress, athletic all-purpose sandals, sleek backpack.

6. Long yoga pants, tank top, cashmere hoodie, quilted winter coat, retro sneakers.

7. Skort, long sleeved yoga-inspired t-shirt, athletic all-purpose sandals.

Blog Posts

Sporty Chic -- Day 1

"Welcome to the world of Sporty Chic"

Moms are the most active group of people on Earth. We do more in a day than most people do in a week. There is no lounging with moms. Lounging stopped when the first contraction started and we haven't sat down since. From the moment we open our eyes in the morning, (or some small person pries our *eyes open for us*) to the moment our heads hit the pillow, moms are on the move.

And yet, somehow this doesn't translate into *fitness*. Somehow, me carrying groceries and bicycles to the car and dancing around like an idiot in Mommy and Me class doesn't give me the six-pack abs I've always hoped for.

That's where Sporty Chic comes in. For many moms, it could very well be the answer to our fashion woes. Sporty Chic takes our day into consideration. The clothes are cute, comfortable and can be thrown in the wash. And you can move in them. If your kid gets stuck in a germ-infested ball pit at fast food restaurant, you can just jump right in and grab them. No need to worry about high heels or dry cleaning bills.

With every outfit this month, I will ask myself –

Do I look sporty without looking like I'm about to actually play a sport?

Am I wearing chic shoes that I can run and play in?

Can this outfit last me all day? Meaning, is the outfit functional enough for the park, yet nice enough to wear out to lunch with friends?

That is the essence of Sporty Chic. Looking active without necessarily being fit. Who knows? Maybe these clothes will have the power to get me to the gym. Or at the very least, get me to buy some *spray tanner...*

Sporty Chic -- Day 4

"How to make a style choice your body isn't ready for"

I must confess I am plagued with a disease that is caused when a too-tired mom sits on the couch *watching* an exercise video while eating cookie batter. I believe the medical term for my problem is called "frontal cottage cheese thighs."

My "F.C.C.T." have never been an issue before this year because I just wore jeans all the time. *Jeans cover everything.* That's why they are the unofficial uniform of moms everywhere. But now that I'm in the midst of my style trial, I can see that years of my sedentary behavior has come home to roost -- right above my knees.

But here's the deal -- dresses are a part of every *style* – there's no getting away from them. And I've discovered that I kind of like wearing dresses as long as they don't reveal my "F.C.C.T". I've started exercising so I know the problem will go away eventually, but until then, what do I do? Do I continue to wear my odd dress/pants combinations? Do I avoid "above the knee" dresses entirely until my legs are ready for public consumption? Do they still make medical support hose in nude? Or should I just wear really short dresses and carry a sign that says, "Pardon my mess -- Legs under construction!" I'm really in a fashion quandary...

Sporty Chic -- Day 5

"Sporty Chic – A style that forces you to exercise"

Sporty Chic style has definitely put me on exercise notice. I've not only joined a gym because of this style, but I've started to look into what I call "Mom Sports". A mom sport is any sport or competition that doesn't require a lot of extra time and learning since we barely have the time to exercise at all, we certainly can't tack on the extra time it takes to research how to *do the exercise*. Take wrestling alligators, for example. Wrestling alligators certainly might be the perfect way to get my thighs ripped (literally), but where do I rent an alligator? Or do I have to buy an alligator? And if I find a great alligator wrestling facility near me, does it have childcare? It's all too much for a busy mom...

So here are some mom sports I've found that are fun, exciting and most moms could jump right into without any prep at all--

The Caber Toss - This is a Scottish sport that involves tossing a large wooden pole called a caber that is approximately nineteen feet long and weighs 175 pounds. *So all you have to do is pick up something heavy and toss it?* Moms carry heavy things all day -- heavy squirming things that are often sticky and crying. I'm betting most moms could toss a caber with a baby *in an ergo carrier on their backs...* and do it all in a sing-songy voice… "Mommy's going to toss the caber now. Let's count together… one, two, three… Mommy tossed the caber! Yay for mommy!"

Curling – This is a sport where players slide stones across a sheet of ice. Two "sweepers" use brooms to sweep the ice in front of the stone to make it go faster. *What mom can't sweep?* I have three kids, three dogs, three cats and a pig that goes in and out of our house all day – just give me a USA jersey and a broom and I could ensure the curling team wins gold at the Olympics.

Race Car Driving – We all know this is a sport where you basically just have to drive really fast and get to the finish line. Well, so what? *You're alone in the car.* I have to drive really fast all the time. But I do it with a carload of kids *while* passing out snacks, adjusting the volume on a story CD and picking up toys that have fallen behind my seat. Moms could easily be racecar drivers. I'm just not sure it would be challenging enough for us.

So those are the "mom sports" I have so far. I'm going to keep researching all month and let you know what I discover. But right now I've got to head to the gym. My Sporty Chic skirt has just informed me that I really need to do some sit-ups and possibly a great deal of squats.

Sporty Chic -- Day 29

"How to wear a dress in a river"

Well, if it's a Sporty Chic dress with that strange, other-worldly quick drying material, just throw it on over a bathing suit, grab an inner tube and jump right in. I got this dress on the clearance rack at Sports Authority in their yoga section. I think it was on the clearance rack because people normally don't do yoga in *dresses*. And it has UV protection just in case you're doing yoga *in a dress in the sun.*

Once again I have to thank Sporty Chic. I spent a great day on the Rainbow River...

Before my month of Sporty Chic I would have thought that scenario could only have been in a bad dream. *You've planned a great day on the river with your family, but for some reason you're in a soaking wet dress, it's see-through, and everyone from high school is watching...*

Sporty Chic -- Day 30

"Sporty Chic, the reckoning"

Today is the last day of June, which means I must say farewell to my Sporty Chic wardrobe. Goodbye to all my razor-back tanks, my dresses that I can wear out to lunch and then go snorkeling in and my cute, insanely durable sandals that will stay attached to my feet under almost any circumstances.

Needless to say, this style brought up a lot of body issues for me. Before this month, I never realized how much I just covered up my dangly parts every day like some modern day Elephant Woman. *"I am not an animal. I am mother of three!"*

At the beginning of this look, I was wearing a dress *with jeans underneath.* How weird is that? But I just couldn't imagine actually showing my legs in public. After years of pregnancies and Pop Tarts, in my mind my legs had become these hideous things that just got me from place to place, like a beat up car I was ashamed of driving. And I didn't just cover up my legs. The first time I walked out of the house in a razor-back tank top with my *upper arms exposed* I felt like I might as well have been topless at a beach in France.

But it felt so liberating to finally throw off my lawn mower tarp and feel the breeze on my limbs again! Is my body exactly how I'd like it to look? No, of course not. But is it as bad as I have built it up in my mind over the years? No, it isn't. No one threw stones at me. No one vomited in their mouth as I passed. And unlike some of my other looks (Mod in particular) my kids *liked all my Sporty Chic outfits.* I don't think they like the outfits so much as they liked *mom in the outfits* – a mom that could easily play tag or wade through a river or go on a bug hunt… A mom that didn't mind getting dirty.

I am so grateful for Sporty Chic. I realized this month how much my body issues have gotten in the way of me playing. How many times since having kids have I just dreaded putting on a bathing suit and going to the pool? How many times have I resisted wearing shorts on a hundred-degree day?

I highly recommend the Sporty Chic look for any mom. Don't let your body issues stop you from trying out this style. Just put the clothes on and go play.

Chapter 9

Mod

Do you like wearing dresses? I mean, do you *really* like wearing dresses? How about skirts? Summer, winter, spring or fall, do you just feel better with those legs of yours dangling out in the breeze? Then Mod is the style for you.

I know what you're thinking – isn't Mod a style from like a thousand years ago? Aren't we talking Twiggy here? Yes, we are. And if you want to get technical, we're talking Mary Quant, the creator of Mod style who just happened to invent the mini skirt. Mod has evolved a lot since those days into a much subtler version of itself. You don't have to wear white go-go boots and a mini dress with a giant bow on it to be Mod anymore -- a tank dress, cute, metallic sandals and some graphic jewelry and you're instantly modern-Mod. And it's such an easy style! You're out the door in five minutes looking polished and adorable. This style, out of all the styles, is meant to be colorful. So have fun with it. Consider yourself a hip mommy rainbow.

Things you'll need:

1. **A-line mini dress** -- Colorful, simple and surprisingly comfortable.

2. **A-line mini skirt** – Can be worn anytime, anywhere. Have some cute leggings on hand to break out when the weather is chilly.

3. **Sailor pants** – The one pair of pants in this look. A simple, fitted black or navy pair works great.

4. **Turtleneck** – A turtleneck has such an awesome 60s vibe, especially when you wear it with a cute mini and boots.

5. **Graphic jewelry** – Go for a big pendant or a chunky bracelet. Not too much though – It's easy to "Mrs. Roper" the jewelry with Mod. (More on that later.)

6. **Sheath dress** – If you think the A-line mini skirt is comfortable, wait until you try the sheath dress. Nothing clings at all and there's no belt.

7. **Trapeze dress** – Sounds weird and too vintage, but they're out there and cute and modern.

8. **Tank dress** – Basically, a large shirt calling itself a dress.

9. **Big patent leather purse** – Mod is a colorful look, so go crazy bright with your purse.

10. **Flat brown boots** – They should hit right below the knee and make sure they don't have a heel.

11. **Fun double-breasted graphic coat** – Look for something that's the same length as your dresses, so they match.

12. **Cap-sleeved blouse** – Silky, can have a little tie front.

13. **Flat colorful sandals** – Strappy or simple. The point is color.

A week of outfits:

1. A-line mini dress, flat colorful sandals, graphic jewelry.

2. Trapeze dress, boots.

3. A-line mini skirt, cap sleeved blouse, flat sandals.

4. Sheath dress, graphic coat, boots.

5. Tank dress, sandals, graphic jewelry.

6. Sailor pants, cap-sleeved blouse, sandals, graphic jewelry.

7. A-line mini skirt, turtleneck, boots.

Blog Posts

Mod -- Day 3

"Stranger danger and Mod"

If Rock & Roll made sketchy people my instant friends and Euro made everyone clear a path and get out of my way, how will *strangers* react to me in Mod?

I become everyone's friend. Yesterday, I felt like Doris Day walking through the grocery store -- Clerks tipping their hats at me, children handing me their balloons, the butcher giving me a wink and a whistle as he weighed my pork loin...

Okay, that exact scenario didn't actually happen. But seriously, strangers haven't struck up this many conversations with me since I was pregnant. And dressing in Mod is better than being pregnant because no creepy person asked to touch my belly.

In our society, we sum up each other *in an instant* by what we're wearing. Overalls? *Farmer.* Teenager in all black? *Troubled.* Guy in a suit? *Business man.* Frazzled woman with bad jeans and big, white sneakers? *Soccer Mom.* Woman with fish net stockings? *Slut.* Woman with no bra and hair armpits? *Hippie slut.*

We need to consider what we are wearing each day because impressions are being made even if we don't realize it. So what does the world think of a woman who is wearing sailor pants, a bright geometric patterned shirt and neon pink purse?

If she's as happy as she dresses, I've just got to say hi...

Mod Day -- Day 5

"Just a girl and her cat"

This dress was an impulse purchase. Before I am convicted in your mind of being completely insane, let me at least describe the circumstances. I was shopping in a 50s/60s vintage store and was surrounded by poodle skirts and small dead animals sewn together as decorative scarves and so when I put this dress on it seemed positively *normal* – like I could wear it in my every day life and no one would bat an eyelash.

Then I brought it home and surrounded by items in *modern times*, this dress seemed quite ridiculous. So I've decided that if I'm questioned about this outfit, I'm going to do one of the following -

A) Just act like people wear this kind of dress all the time.

B) Lie and say I'm headed to a 60s costume party.

C) Pretend I'm an "adult child" on a field trip outing with other members of my group home. I'll store a yo-yo and a giant rainbow lollipop in my purse just in case.

Or perhaps, under no circumstances will I ever leave the perimeter of my property with this garment on.

Mod -- Day 8

"The Mrs. Roper Effect"

I have always been slightly wary of costume jewelry. I've seen it on other people and thought, *Wow, that looks so cute, stylish and fun.* I really should get some costume jewelry and then I will be cute, stylish and fun. Who knows? Maybe wearing costume jewelry will be the start of a whole new me. Maybe I'll even learn an instrument like the fiddle or an obscure language. People will ask, *Why did you learn Finnish?* And I will say, Olen söpö, tyylikäs ja hauska. (Because I am cute, stylish and fun).

So I finally got some costume jewelry and I have to say, I don't look cute, stylish or fun. *I look like Mrs. Roper from Three's Company.*

Beware of Mod jewelry and the *Mrs. Roper effect*. Mod jewelry is meant to be big, bold and colorful and it's often plastic. I have only received compliments from my daughter about my Mod jewelry and although I trust her taste in clothes, her taste in jewelry is something entirely different. It's hard to take jewelry compliments seriously from someone who is wearing a paperclip necklace and holding a wand.

So go ahead and get some cute, stylish and fun costume jewelry. It's great for moms because it's cheap and if it breaks, no biggie, but hold back on the *amount* you wear in single day. As they say in Finland, Lapissa poroja on vain harvoilla soittaa kelloja. (Lapland reindeer need only few bells).

Mod -- Day 14

"The many uses of a cowl neck sweater"

I must confess, I've always known what a cowl neck collar looked like, but until recently (like moments ago when I Googled it) I thought they were actually called *cow* necks. This never made any sense to me because it seemed a rather unflattering term for a piece of clothing. What does a big, floppy collar have to do with *farming*? But I never questioned it.

After all, I'm sure the experts in the *naming* department at Fashion Head-quarters (which is located in a super secret bubble under the ocean) know what they're doing.

So when I bought this cute, Mod-inspired, cowl neck sweater at a consignment store the other day, I looked it up to get its history by just typing in "cow necks" and got a bunch of pictures of actual cows with bells around their necks. I not only discovered my mistake, but learned about some dairy farming traditions in Bhutan.

Yesterday, I put on a cowl neck sweater, skinny jeans and boots and I was feeling pretty good. After a few days of fashion blunders it felt great to be wearing something I felt confident in. I grabbed my purse, my children and my coffee and headed to the car giving one last big scratch as I always do to our pig, Hogan, and even bent down into his face to tell him how much I loved him … and that's when *he sneezed in my eye.*

Now a pig sneeze is not a dainty sneeze. It's not like a fly sneeze or even a cat sneeze, done with relative quiet and very little output. A pig sneeze is like being hit at a hundred miles an hour with a cup of hot, slimy oatmeal. In addition to snot, it has dirt in it because Hogan spends his days digging everything up in our yard that is pretty. So the sneeze not only has volume, *it has weight.*

I stumbled backward blindly, shouting for my kids to help. Very much like the time I ran to them for assistance when I had a bunch of yellow jackets stuck in my hair, my kids did nothing except run inside the house and research foster care families they would prefer to live with.

On my own and still blind, I started scooping the snot out of my eye the best I could and when that didn't seem to be working, I used *my cowl neck sweater.*

It was just the amount of fabric needed for the job, which proves that after all these years of calling it the wrong name, I was still somewhat right. These collars were meant for the farm.

Mod --Day 27

"Mod and Tim McGraw"

Emboldened by InStyle Magazine's stark prediction of an all-Mod future, I decided to spend the final days of March in all my *extreme Mod clothes* to give myself the best possible whack at the style to see if it worked on me. Who knows? Maybe it's like vegetables or exercise or reading The Berenstain Bears "Learn about Strangers" to your kids. You have to do it a lot to really see any benefits. (Except for the Berenstain Bears book which you could read a million times to your kids and they'd only really learn what to do if a strange *bear* approached them and asked them to get into a car. And what child in their right mind would go anywhere with a *talking bear* in the first place? Let alone one behind the wheel of a car? *The book has no foundation in logic.)*

So here's extreme Mod outfit #1.

Okay, I agree this outfit is a little crazy – and somewhere inside me I knew that all day. But it must be the same feeling you get when you find out you only have a few days to live. I knew I'd NEVER wear the outfit again, *so I just appreciated every little detail about it.* My cold arms... The itchy linen material... The ever-painful red ballet flats... The way the dress clung to my hips in all the wrong ways... And of course, the white tights that grabbed dirt and globs of hair as if they were magnetic...

It's like that Tim McGraw song, "Live Like You Were Dying." And don't pretend you're too cool *not* to know what song I'm talking about or that you've never cried along with it in the car at least ONCE. It goes something like this -- "I went skydiving, rocky mountain climbing, I went 8.2 hours in a dress called Pan Am Stewardess."

And just like the song says, "I hope you all someday get the chance to dress like you were dying.to *dress like you were dying...*

Mod -- Day 30

"The hottest outfit on Earth"

And by hot, I don't mean sexy. I am using hot in the traditional sense of the word as in hot, boiling, dripping with sweat and babbling incoherently due to heat. I found this cute, vintage, Mod dress and I just loved it. Easy to wear and it even comes with its own belt. Just throw on some white tights and black boots and off I go.... to sweat like I have the flu. It's one hundred percent polyester. I didn't exactly understand the term "breathable fabric" until I wore this little number and experienced unbreathable fabric. It was kind of cold yesterday, about fifty degrees, and when I walked out of the house I didn't feel cold at all – that should have been my first red flag. *What a great dress*, I thought. *No coat necessary.*

Then I headed somewhere no one should ever go in a hundred percent polyester anything – a toddler music class. By the time my son and I sang the "Hello" song, I knew my natural deodorant was a poor choice for me. By the time we were all dancing around pretending to be ponies, sweat was running down my back and I was nauseating other parents. And by the time we all were singing "Shoo fly, don't bother me" I was shooing actual flies away from me.

So all in all, it's a very cute and very deadly dress. What a shame. I love this dress, but I'm loathe to put it on again unless I really need to lose a lot of water weight fast, I'm going ice fishing and need something warm to wear or I have to melt some petroleum for an oil lamp in my armpits.

A word about jobs...

Obviously, your job is a huge factor in finding your style. If you're a stay-at-home mom, you can blast through your style trial without any interruptions. But it gets trickier for a working mom. I'm a working mom, but since I work from home I could wear a clown suit every day and never get fired. But *going* to work every day is totally different. There are expectations of how you should look that you're going to need to consider when sampling different styles. Maybe you have a great job in a totally accepting place that will delight in your schizophrenic weekly wardrobe changes. Maybe an office pool will get started on what style you're going to eventually pick. Chances are you'll even inspire other people in your office to go on their own style quests.

Of course, that would be the ideal situation. But you might not have a job like that. You might have a job where you are expected to look a certain way. If your job is an airline safety inspector, I doubt they'd like you showing up suddenly dressed like a Slacker. If you're a lawyer and you have a big trial, you might not want to appear in court in torn fishnets and a Marilyn Manson t-shirt.

In fact, you might have to keep your office "uniform" and just have your own personal style at home and on the weekends. I can't really help you in this department. These are style waters you're going to have to navigate on your own. However, if for some reason your style trial does get you into trouble at work, you're welcome to have your boss call me. I can be really angry, meek or apologetic, depending on what's necessary. I'm also not above name-calling. And if you do get fired, just shout very loudly as you're leaving the office, "Hey, more time to shop!"

Chapter 10

Artsy Mom

Most moms are considered anything but artsy. Deep thoughts, we don't have. But compared to the rest of society, we actually do have huge existential issues we wrestle with on a daily basis. *Where am I going? Is this all there is? Am I more than just a mom?* We're basically a bunch of Nietzsches in minivans and no one knows that. But if you dress in Artsy Mom, everyone will know.

Artsy Mom, like Euro, is a formidable look. The Artsy Mom looks as if she drops by a modern art museum as often as most people drop by the grocery. Dress as an Artsy Mom and people will assume you have a degree in Art History even if you said to hell with education by third grade. The Artsy Mom look is polished, but edgy. A black suit with an interesting necklace, an asymmetrical blouse with a zippered mini skirt, a shirt with big butterfly sleeves and a pair of tailored men's pants... It's not about picking up a few plaid shirts at The Gap and calling it a day. It's about thinking of clothes *as art*. Artsy Mom is a style and concept all in one.

You probably know what I'm going to say here, but I'll say it anyway. This is not a style for anyone with children under five. A black suit and a baby is a recipe for disaster unless it's a black Hazmat suit. However, if you have tweens, teenagers or beyond -- you've got to try this style. It will scare, impress and intimidate your teenager's friends, which is the best way of scaring, intimidating and impressing your teenager. And an impressed teenager just might be more apt to do their chores and be seen with you in public.

Things you'll need:

1. *Black suit* – Feminine cut. Remember, this is Artsy Mom, not "Men in Black 4".

2. *Asymmetrical top* – The bottom or the top of the shirt can be asymmetrical, either way is cool and edgy.

3. **Artsy jewelry** – This is where you really highlight the concept of clothes as art. Wear the most interesting pieces of jewelry you can find. Jewelry can be big or small – just think unconventional.

4. **Pointy black ankle boots** – With a high, sleek heel.

5. **Gunmetal silky sleeveless shirt** – You can find one with a collar or without. Get one that's a little longer so you have the option of tucking it in or letting it be all flowy.

6. **Funky asymmetrical dress** – Think cocktail party at the Guggenheim.

7. **White silk tank** – Can be worn with everything. You'll need a cami underneath so it's not see-through.

8. **Wide leg menswear trousers** -- These can look really androgynous. The Artsy Mom is never concerned about impressing the male gender with what she's wearing. Love her for her brain or don't love her at all.

9. **Shirt with crazy butterfly sleeves** – These shirts look like regular shirts until you pick your arm up and then, WOW. Do a lot of pointing and giving directions when wearing this shirt.

10. **Large black patent leather purse** – Simple and elegant, but large enough to hold a soccer ball or architectural plans.

11. **Strappy metallic sandals** – Try to find some that are interesting and artsy. Shoes are another place the Artsy Mom can show off her unusual taste.

12. **Zippered black mini** – Adds a little funk to an otherwise polished wardrobe.

① ② ④ ③ ⑥ ⑤

A week of outfits:

1. Black suit, white silky blouse, pointy black ankle boots, artsy jewelry.

2. Shirt with crazy butterfly sleeves, zippered black mini, strappy metallic sandals.

3. Menswear trousers, Gunmetal silky sleeveless shirt, pointy black ankle boots.

4. Funky asymmetrical dress, pointy black ankle boots, artsy jewelry.

5. Asymmetrical top, menswear trousers, metallic sandals.

6. Black suit, gunmetal sleeveless top, strappy ankle sandals.

7. Zippered mini, white silky tank, pointy black ankle boots, artsy jewelry.

Blog Posts

Artsy Mom -- Day 5

"The Artsy Mom word for the day – unapproachable"

You can smile all you want, but dressed in Artsy Mom the world will just see you as an ice queen. Here are some of the things I heard about this outfit –

"I feel intimidated talking to you when you're dressed like that."

"If you were wearing that outfit when we met, I don't think we would have become friends."

"I was wondering who that person was dressed up like *that*, then I realized it was you!"

Maybe part of the issue is that I'm wearing black in the country.

Country people still only wear black for funerals. If I lived in a city I would totally blend in with everyone else. Although the good news is, as far as the service industry goes, I'm back in Euro territory. Whether I'm standing in line at the toy store or getting my fourth latte for the day, salespeople scramble to help me. When I was dressed in Euro, I got great service because people assumed I was rich. But with Artsy Mom, it doesn't feel like that. It feels like I'm getting great service because, judging by the way I'm dressed, I'm the type of person that *if I don't get great service*, I will throw a foot-stomping fit. So Artsy Mom definitely has its perks. Which means I am so wearing this outfit the next time I go to the DMV.

Artsy Mom -- Day 17

"An Artsy Mom goes to the style mother ship"

My family and I went to a modern art museum in San Francisco today and it was like going to the Artsy Mom style mother ship. There were women crawling all over the museum dressed in their artsy best – long dramatic coats, pointy severe eyewear and extreme jewelry. I felt like I not only blended in with the pack, but that I was even dressed on the *boring side*. I could have gone supreme artsy, even supreme Avant-Garde and no one would have even batted a heavily mascara-ed eyelash.

What a difference location makes on style. Halfway through the exhibits I noticed that I was dragging a piece of hay on one of my sandals. Artsy Mom style is great but will my country location doom our love affair? It gets dirty so easily and the clothes are just not that kid-friendly. After I pulled the hay off my sandals (after closer examination I noticed there was a lot more than just one piece), I also saw some candy on my shirt -- I think it was the remnant of a Dum Dum lollipop -- which means most of my outfit is now headed to the dry cleaners.

I know there are people out there that dress completely the opposite of their surroundings, but I also know that if I'm going to shed my former sloppy self and become stylish from now on, it has to be *easy*. And by that I mean I have to be able to find all the clothes for my look *around where I live*, they must be *inexpensive* and they must be able to take *a big dirt punch*. I can't resist a hug from one of my sticky kids just because I'm wearing an antique taffeta halter-top. So Artsy Mom is still getting a question mark in my book. My investigation will continue the rest of the month, but for now I'm going to bed, tired, momentarily hay and lollipop free and happily full of art...

Artsy Mom -- Day 30

"Lessons I've learned from Artsy Mom"

Today is the last day of Artsy Mom and my final photo for this look only seems fitting –

I'm bowling… in an Artsy Mom outfit… with bowling shoes…

Do Artsy Moms bowl? *Probably not.* Do Artsy Moms go to water parks with their kids? *It's unlikely.* Do Artsy Moms carry goats out of their houses that have broken in through the front door? *I'm going to go out on a limb here and say no.* Do Artsy Moms do any of the things that I do on a daily basis? No.

I had a lot of fun with this look. It's an empowering look – bold, in your face and edgy – words most moms would not use to describe themselves. I didn't feel like a mom in these clothes and that was a very refreshing feeling. Don't get me wrong, I love being a mom, I just don't like looking like a mom.

For the first time in a long while, I was dressing for me and not just dressing for practicality. These clothes reminded me that I have thoughts other than how to pack a healthy lunch and when to get my kids to school on time. This look reminded me that I am a person alone in this world, on my own adventure and that even though my focus is taking care of three other people, *I'm still the star of my own movie.*

So for that, Artsy Mom, I thank you.

Chapter 11

Gamine

What's Gamine, anyway? Is it a country in Africa? Is it a nail polish color? Is it an illness you get from sitting on a public toilet seat? No, it's actually a style – a French style, specifically. Gamine means *urchin* in French and it's a look that blends the masculine and feminine. Am I losing you? Okay, just think Audrey Hepburn. She's the icon for this style. Or just think about yourself peddling to the market on a vintage bicycle to pick up your daily baguette – that's Gamine.

In addition to being just a freaking adorable look, Gamine has some features that any mom would love –

No high heels – Mostly sandals and ballet flats. Nothing, I repeat, NOTHING uncomfortable.

Sweater sets – Sweater sets? Yes, they still exist and paired with Capri pants and ballet flats, you can get dressed in under five minutes and still manage to look cute. Sweater sets are also great at hiding the mom pooch and unfortunate, dangling, "Wave good-bye arms."

Big cotton underwear – I don't know about you, but now that I'm a mom, the thong ship has sailed for me. Really, why would I want to *purposely* display my cellulite? And yet, I feel kind of guilty about this – like, *Shouldn't I still be trying to wear sexy underwear?* Fortunately, because Gamine is such a girly look, you can settle right into a pair of big, ol' cotton undies knowing that you're not only comfortable, but also completely stylish. *Hello, Fruit of the Loom? I'd like to buy a twelve pack.*

Pixie Hair – Gamines love short, cropped, boyish haircuts and if you think about it, what better hair style to have as a mom? No hair dryers, no styling required and best of all, no mom ponytail. You barely have to wash this haircut and it looks super cute.

Add some dainty jewelry and Gamine style will turn you instantly into the cutest thing on the planet. People will actually stop looking at your children and just look at you – that's how cute you're going to look.

Things you'll need:

1. **Breton striped top** – Otherwise known as a French sailor shirt. There are lots of different color combinations out there, but go for the classic navy and white.

2. **Skinny belt** – Understated, simple.

3. **Tan trench coat** – A Breton striped top under a classic trench coat? You are officially French, bébé!

4. **Pedal pushers** – These are cute pants that hit right below the knee.

5. **Bubble mini skirt** – The bubble mini turns a regular outfit into a party-worthy ensemble.

6. **A-line mini skirt** – Schoolgirl cute.

7. **Straw bag** – Try to get one that's cloth-lined. They seem to last longer and don't scratch up the things you're carrying.

8. **Patent leather ballet flats** – Shiny red are so chic.

9. **Dainty sweater** – Can be worn draped over the shoulders or buttoned up. A sweater set works here too.

10. **Beret** – Or a newsboy cap. The point is to finish off your outfit with a cute little hat.

11. **Flat strappy sandals** – Very different from the flat, strappy sandals in Artsy Mom. The Gamine strappy sandal can be either a classic pair of espadrilles or a canvas sling back.

12. **Flowered scoop neck t-shirts** -- This is your go-to t-shirt. Pick up a few plain scoop neck t-shirts in different colors while you're at it.

A week of outfits:

1. Breton striped top, pedal pushers, skinny belt, trench coat, red ballet flats.

2. Flowered scoop neck, bubble mini, strappy sandals, cute hat.

3. A-line mini skirt, Breton striped top, skinny belt, espadrilles.

4. Sweater set, pedal pushers, ballet flats, cute hat.

5. A-line mini skirt, plain scoop neck t-shirt, ballet flats, dainty sweater.

6. Flowered scoop neck t-shirt, pedal pushers, skinny belt, espadrilles, trench coat.

7. Bubble mini, scoop neck t-shirt, flat strappy sandals.

Blog Posts

Gamine --Day 6

"How to get creepy men to notice you"

I wore this Gamine-ish outfit to Costco yesterday and there I was minding my own business just buying my usual forty gallons of soy sauce when I happened to glance over a tube sock hill. I noticed a man staring at me. And not just staring, but checking me out... actually leering...

No one ever leers at me. Not in the past, not in the present and certainly not at Costco. I am not the type of woman men leer at and *I like it that way.* I disregarded the incident and moved on and no sooner was I standing in the check out line when I caught another man leering at me.

That's when I realized what it was – my Gamine outfit. Some men must really go for that sweet, innocent, girlish thing – I believe they're called pedophiles. It happened again with another man as I was leaving. I started thinking I was crazy. Maybe it wasn't my Gamine outfit. Maybe there was a support group meeting at Costco. I looked around for any sign that might say, "Welcome Pedophiles of the North Bay" but found nothing.

As I drove home and pondered my experience I realized that a certain type of guy must be drawn to a woman in a sweater set and headband, and not necessarily just a pedophile. If Euro style says "I'm better" and Rock & Roll style says "Don't mess with me", then Gamine just might say, "I'm sweet. I have no opinions. I just like to smile and have really good posture and agree with whatever you say."

Yuck. I didn't think guys like that existed anymore, but I guess they do. And apparently, they shop at Costco. Today my kids and I are headed to the Jelly Bean Factory. I wonder what weirdos I'll find there.

Gamine -- Day 10

"A Gamine takes on illness"

On Thursday night, after a full day at Lake Tahoe with my B.F.F. Apryl and our combined five children, I finally put my kids to bed about nine, poured myself a glass of wine and hunkered down in front of the hotel room's flat screen to watch *The Girl with the Dragon Tattoo.*

Pajamas, thick socks, alcohol and Daniel Craig. It was pure bliss. And just as I'm about at the part where Daniel Craig and Rooney Mara are going to hook up, I heard one of my kids crying…. and then the unmistakable sounds of vomit hitting the floor.

Good God, no, I thought. Please don't tell me. I couldn't have heard that right. And then I heard it again. But this time the splashing sounded more muffled, like it was hitting the sheets. And sure enough, August had the stomach flu and spent most of the night trying to do as much damage to our hotel room as possible. Little kids don't get that "I feel like I'm about to be sick so I should head to the bathroom" thing, so it was pretty much *Exorcist* time. I ran out of towels about midnight. I ran out of pajamas (for both of us) about three. I ran out of the will to live about five.

The only outfit I had for our five hour drive home was a skirt, silky top and heels – not a great outfit if you've had no sleep and are feeling a little nauseous yourself. Here we are at check-out –

Look how happy and perky August and I look! And as you can see, everyone else seems really concerned that the two of us aren't doing well. Shortly after this picture was taken, I pushed the cart down the ramp in the front of the hotel and it tipped over, spilling all the contents over (except August who hung on) in front of the valet stand. Strangers had to pick up our bread, oranges and bathing suits.

Ahhhh, just another day in the fabulous life of a Gamine...

Gamine -- Day 13

"The pitfalls of Gamine style"

Okay, I totally hate this outfit. When I first put it on yesterday morning, I thought, *Wow, I am so Gamine... Look at me, world! Drink in my innocence and naiveté!* I actually never gave one single thought to whether I liked the outfit or not. I just felt like, mission accomplished. But as the day wore on I began to realize how much I hated the outfit. It wasn't really how the outfit looked (which wasn't that bad), but how the outfit made me feel. How frumpy I felt. How lame. How prim. I mean, seriously, where are my "Church of Latter Day Saints" pamphlets? Where is my car with the bumper sticker that says, "Have you hugged your wheaten terrier today?"

I've said this before, but clothes have the power to seriously influence my mood and how I feel about myself. And by the end of the day, I wanted to burn this outfit, throw on an Iron Maiden t-shirt and bite the head off of a chicken.

I guess when you make a false move in Gamine style, you land right in a P.T.A. meeting. Be afraid... Be very afraid...

Gamine -- Day 15

"Hello, I'm wearing a hat"

I decided to wear a hat all day for several reasons –

1) *Without the hat, the outfit had no real chance of looking Gamine.*

2) *I never wear hats, so I thought I'd see what it felt like to wear one all day.*

3) *After about an hour of wearing a hat, I had such bad "hat hair" that I couldn't take it off.*

People loved the hat. I mean, seriously, I got an insane amount of compliments over just some thing I stuck on my head. But I had a hard time focusing on conversations because of the constant internal dialogue I could not seem to turn off in my head.

Conversations would go like this --

Person: *Hi, Holly. How are you?*

Me: *Great. How are you? (Did you notice I'm wearing a hat? We're indoors, and yet I'm wearing a hat. Isn't that weird?)*

Person: *Did you have a nice summer?*

Me: *We had such a fun summer. How about you? (I'm still wearing a hat and still indoors. In fact, I've just noticed I'm the only one indoors with a hat on.)*

Person: *We had a fun summer too. I can't believe school is starting next week.*

Me: *I know. It feels like the kids just got out of school. (How can you even talk to me and not see that I'm wearing a hat?)*

Person: *By the way, I love your hat.*

Me: *What? Oh, this thing? I forgot I even had it on... (Okay, so it is weird that I'm wearing a hat. I knew it.)*

I'm working my way up to a beret. I can already hear the shouting match I'm going to have in my head over that one.

Gamine -- Day 31

"Good-bye Gamine. It's been sweet"

It is the last day of August, which means it's my last day of Gamine. Gone are the days of sweater sets and espadrilles. Gone are the days of poorly executed ponytails and pearl earrings. Gone are the days of trying to mimic French insouciance.

Ultimately, Gamine is too nice of a look for me. And I don't mean nice as in *fancy,* I mean nice, as in, it's a style meant for nice people. Even more specifically, *sweet* people. And I'm just not that sweet, really, ask anyone. And that's okay because I'm not really going for sweet. There are other adjectives I'm more interested in attaining -- kind, generous, thoughtful, smart, funny, interesting. But sweet? Homecoming queens can keep that one.

But as with all my months, I've managed to take away something really valuable from Gamine -- just like Sporty Chic taught me that I could reveal more of my legs than just my ankles and my month of Maxi Dresses taught me how incredibly easy and comfortable it is to wear a dress around all day -- *Gamine taught me about hats.* And I don't mean the newsboy hats that I tried and failed with, but sun hats.

A cute sun hat is thing to behold. It transforms a boring outfit into something great. It dresses up a sloppy outfit and makes an already dressy outfit fun. Oh yeah, it also keeps the sun off your face. Why I spent my entire life wandering around outside with a baseball cap on is a mystery to me. Those days are over. I am all about the chic sun hat now.

Which I think is sooooo sweet.

Chapter 12

Hippie

When you just read "Hippie", what was the image that came to your mind? A mom with no bra and lots of armpit hair? Or maybe that mom at the park who drinks really nasty looking teas and still breastfeeds her ten year old? That's definitely a *type* of hippie and I would never make fun of her or her homemade granola bars and non-effective crystal rock deodorant. But what I'm talking about is a different type of hippie– a *modern* hippie whose style is earthy and carefree, but definitely polished.

I love this style. This is the style I chose after My Year of Fabulous. It has everything I'm looking for in an everyday wardrobe. 1. The clothes are very wash-and-wear and even what I call "barf-friendly". 2. Everything is pretty, but not fussy. 3. The footwear is all boots or Birkenstocks. 4. Since I live in the hippie Mecca of Northern California, I can find everything I need at consignment or thrift stores for cheap, cheap, cheap. 5. Best of all, this look tells the world that I'm a happy, easygoing, non-conformist – which is kind of what I am. This look says, "If you'd like to talk about the evils of plastic bags and great hiking spots, I'm your gal. But if you need someone to be in charge of the May Faire committee at school, I would be a very bad choice."

So if you're the kind of mom I am, this style might just be the one for you.

Things you'll need:

1. ***Bell Bottom jeans*** -- Don't buy a pair that has gigantic bells – it looks too costumey and they're really annoying to walk in. If you can fit a cat up your pants, the bells are too big.

2. ***Wrap sweater*** – Go big and cozy and look for the kind that have a tie belt. Think, *What would I wear to a bonfire?*

3. ***Denim cut-offs*** – You can wear some that hit just above the knee, but short-shorts are technically better.

4. *Skinny khaki pants* – Flat front. Can be worn with boots, moccasins or Birkenstocks.

5. *Faded low-rise jeans* – Different from the bells. You can't wear bells every day.

6. *Peasant skirt* – Channel Stevie Nicks on this one.

7. *Flowing jersey dress* – Big, drapey, flowy awesomeness.

8. *Tunic* – Look for an Indian tunic that isn't crazy bejeweled. Another version of the tunic is a peasant shirt. Scoring both would be ideal.

9. *Colorful t-shirts* – Slim-fitting, cotton.

10. *Aviator sunglasses* – Aviators come in different sizes, so make sure you find some that fit your face. You don't want to look like a giant bug.

11. *Gladiator sandals* – I love gladiator sandals because they zip up the back and actually stay on your feet.

12. *Birkenstock sandals* – My go-to summer sandal. I buy a new pair every summer in a different color, so I have an army of these shoes.

13. *Fringy ankle boots* – So Sacagawea.

14. *Dainty gold necklace* – I like dainty jewelry for the hippie look because it balances the big and flowing aspect of this style. If I'm wearing a big hippie dress and big, chunky jewelry, I feel like a bag lady.

15. *Slouchy hobo bag* – Hard to find things in, but you're a hippie so you won't care.

16. *Vintage leather flower belt* – Thick ones are so 60s Woodstock.

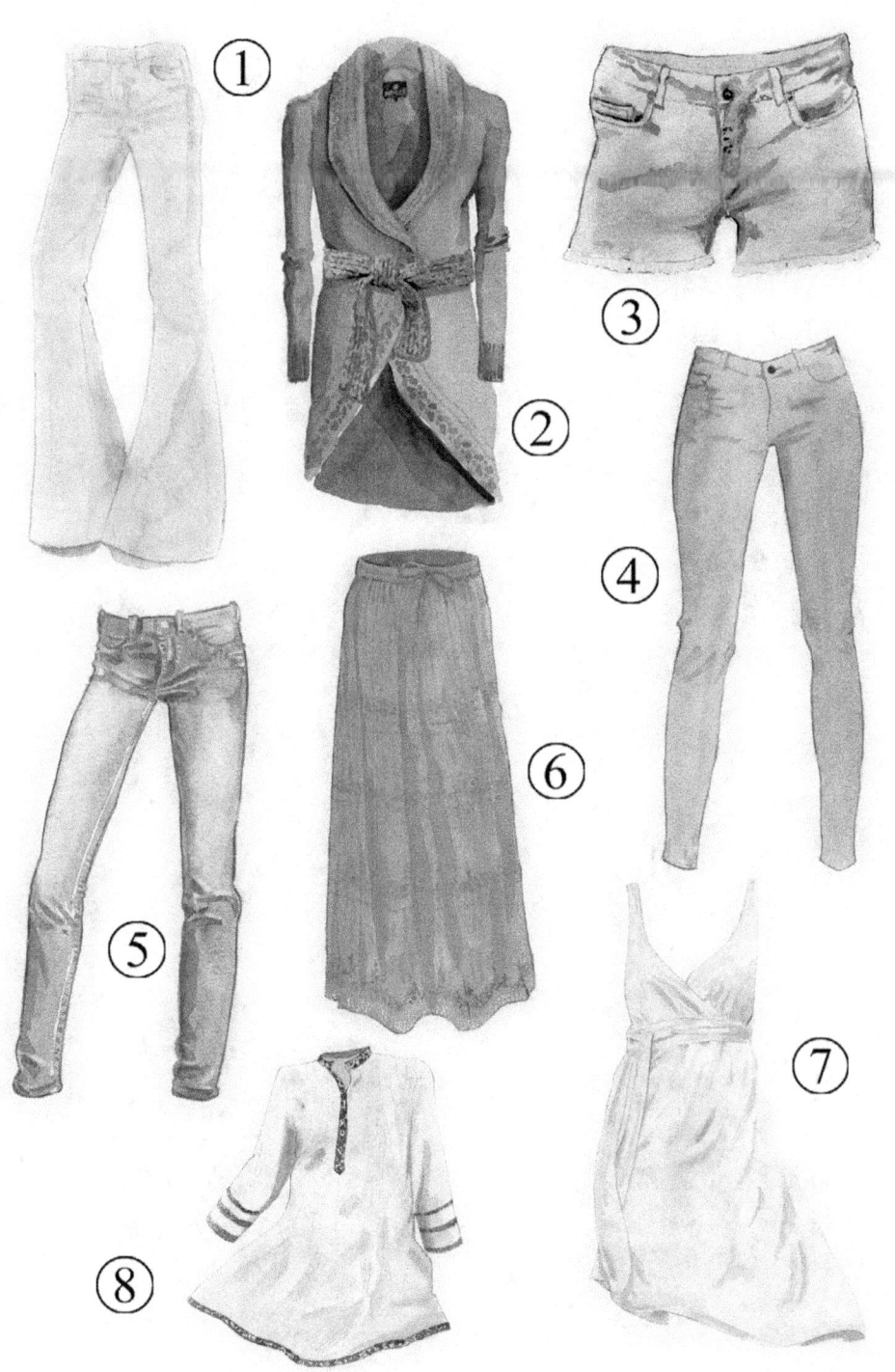

A week of outfits:

1. Tunic, soft faded low-rise jeans, gladiator sandals, hobo bag.

2. Jersey dress, gladiator sandals, dainty jewelry, aviators.

3. Bell Bottom jeans, slim-fitting colorful t-shirt, wrap sweater, Birkenstocks.

4. Peasant skirt, colorful t-shirt, gladiator sandals, vintage leather flower belt.

5. Peasant shirt, skinny khaki pants, aviators, fringy boots, dainty jewelry.

6. Denim cut-off shorts, vintage leather flower belt, colorful t-shirt, hobo bag, Birkenstocks.

7. Tunic, skinny khaki pants, Birkenstocks, aviators.

Blog Posts

Hippie -- Day 1

"Say hello to a carefree Hippie mom"

Oh, how lucky it is to be a hippie. Hippie women dance by themselves at parties. They don't wear bras because they *need* to, but only if they *want* to. They hitchhike without fear of being bludgeoned with a hammer. I have great admiration for the hippie. It's a sexy look without showing a lot of skin. This look says, "I never get flu shots and yet I never get the flu." This look says, "When I vote at all, I vote for vegans." The hippie has inner confidence. The hippie takes the road less travelled.

Hippie is a great look for *moms* because –

Hippies are okay with chaos. *So instead of kicking yourself because your house is a disaster, your hippie look will remind you to take a deep breath and have a hot cup of herbal tea. Or maybe a pot cookie.*

Hippie works for any body type. *Everything is so long and flowy, you can let your freak c-section mom body fly.*

Hippie boasts a lot of flowery prints. *Prints that hide peanut butter and jelly stains.*

I am so excited about being a hippie for a month. As a tightly wound individual, I'm always looking for ways to unwind. I've tried everything, but I'm too hyper to meditate and I certainly don't have time for ninety minutes of yoga every morning. I'm thinking if I just dress like someone who meditates and does yoga, maybe a calm serenity will wash over me. My only concern is that "hippie" is not known for responsibility. You will never hear the phrase, "I have the best hippie financial planner." So what if the look takes me so far into carefree land that I lose myself completely, forget to pay the bills and pick up my children from school because I'm having too much fun staring at a leaf?

Only time will tell. Although, I won't know what time it is because hippies don't wear watches.

Wish me luck. Or maybe just send me some good vibes.

Hippie -- Day 2

"Let your clothes de-stress you"

One of the great things about trying out a brand new style every month is how the world seems so bright, shiny and exciting on a regular basis. This never happens as an adult -- you get to be a whole new person on the first of every month! It's like having New Year's Day twelve times a year and all the terrible things you did the previous year. You just say to yourself, *So what if I gained a hundred pounds, alienated most of my friends with my abusive tirades, gambled away my house in a poorly played game of Whack-a-Mole and ran something over with my car that was quite large and wearing a jogging suit – that was last year.* This year is going to be different because I'm going to be a different person.

Yesterday, I started my new hippie look. Sure, Mod was difficult. Mod was embarrassing. Mod made me want to get in a time machine and go back and kill the person who invented polyester. But Mod is over and now everything is going to be different because I am a free-lovin', travel-by-the-seat-of-my-pants, patchouli stinkin' hippie.

Did it bother me that my child was running around in music class like a wild animal while all the other children were sitting politely singing songs? *Not at all, man. The hippie mom lets their children express themselves however they feel they need to.*

Did it bother me that my paper bag of groceries split open on the way to the car and all my local, organic, seasonal, slow-food products rolled all over the street? *Not in the slightest. The hippie shopper knows when the Earth is giving them a little instant Karma reminder that one should always bring their re-usable, hemp-made bags to the grocery store.*

Did it bother me that my hippie wrap skirt blew open in front of the library exposing my nether-regions to a group of horrified passerbys? *Actually, yes, very much so. If I had a hippie shovel, I would have dug a hole in our precious Earth and jumped inside.*

But all in all, I am very excited about the new me in my new look. It was a good day, and I think it will be a very good month to be a hippie.

Hippie -- Day 5

"How to buy a goat"

We'd all love to have goats, but so many of us don't want to go through the effort of maintaining them... until now. In my month of wearing hippie style clothes, I'm making every effort to also embody the hippie *lifestyle*. That means eating all organic, healthy food (check!), being out in nature whenever possible (check!), having a spontaneous and care-free attitude (on most days, check!) and randomly buying farm animals off Craigslist (double check)!

We bought goats yesterday and the pre-hippie me would have done tireless research on goats *before* buying them, chatted on goat-loving websites, checked out tons of goat books from the library and of course, set up proper fencing so that the goats wouldn't eat our house and cars and everything we love once they arrived.

But not the hippie me. The hippie me trusts the universe. The hippie me would rather spend my time dancing or making jam rather than reading some dumb, old book. And even though we've only had our goats a few hours, I thought I'd pass on what I've learned...

How to buy a goat hippie-style:

1. Sure, there are a lot of different breeds of goats out there and some may suit your needs better than others, but really, who cares? Just find a goat on Craigslist. I found goats with this simple, yet horrifying description: "Baby goats for sale – for soup or BBQ."

2. Get as little information over the phone as possible – Don't ask questions like, "What kind are they?" "How will I get them home?" or "Do they have any diseases?" Don't be a goat buzz-kill.

3. Take as many children as possible with you so that you can ensure chaos will reign on the ride home. I waited until my children had two friends over so that made a grand total of five children and two goats in my car on the freeway ride home – that is what I call hippie mom fun! Also, having extra children will ensure ear-splitting screams as goats start urinating in the car.

4. Get ready for a fast learning curve as you enter into the wonderful, unexpected world of goats – like, they have horns and can blind you easily if you're holding them close to your face.

5. And finally, introduce your wary husband to the goats the moment they begin to pull the insulation out from under the house. He'll love to see all his hard homeowner work being admired by your new, cloven-footed friends.

That's all so far. These new, I-have-no-idea-what-kind-of-goats have been rescued from the soup pot and are happily wreaking havoc at their new home and all is good in my hippie world.

Hippie -- Day 6

"Mom conspiracies uncovered"

It was a fairly even split on my furry sweater – some people found it delightfully fun while others swore they saw a pair of eyes peering out from beneath the fur, watching my every move… waiting for me to let my guard down for just a second… These split opinions helped me so much in defining my existence as a hippie this month. I discovered that if someone tells me they think what I'm wearing is awful, my inner hippie doesn't get mad, hurt or insecure. My inner hippie values all opinions, but none above my own. And this is very different than how I usually feel about my clothes, which is if someone even gives them a strange *glance*, I will quickly second guess my entire outfit, drive to a thrift store, throw the clothes out the window, then drive home naked. So because my pimped out furry sweater makes me happy, my inner hippie has instructed me to keep wearing it.

Another opinion that helped cement who I am as a hippie was the extremely paranoid *something is living in your sweater* comment. That's when I realized what kind of hippie I truly am… and that is a conspiracy-loving one. There are, of course, the classic conspiracies – fake moon landing, Kennedy assassination, Area 51 – all awesome and all *totally true*. But I've recently uncovered a few *mom* conspiracies that I'd like to share with you -- designed to drive all moms slowly insane...

1. *Why is it that the same jeans you wore to the hospital when you were in labor suddenly don't fit when you want to wear them home again? How can you be fatter after you've had the baby? Because your jeans were switched to smaller jeans when you weren't looking. It's a conspiracy by mega "legging" corporations to turn you into a sad shell of your former self, also know as "stretch pants mom."*

2. *Why is it that babies only seem to want to take naps in moving cars? Simple. They are genetically engineered to do so by oil companies through our prenatal vitamins.*

3. *Why is it that husbands seem to have no idea how the washing machine works or that a bathing suit top and a tutu don't qualify as proper school attire? I have no idea, but I'm sure it's a conspiracy.*

4. *Why is everyone so mean and awful to me while I have PMS? Conspiracy.*

5. *Why is it that the one time I make it to a spinning class at the gym, I am stuck between two perfectly dressed, amazing looking women that seem to think they are competing in the Tour de France? This is a conspiracy by Lance Armstrong to remind people how hard cycling really is and why don't you just try and win the Tour de France seven times without taking drugs if you think it's so easy...*

6. *Why are the straws on those little Horizon milks so short that your kids lose them inside the drink within three seconds of being opened? Conspiracy by cows to remind us that cow's milk is actually intended for baby cows...*

...And those are off the top of my hippie head. As the month goes on and I start experimenting with recreational drugs, I'm sure I'll come up with more conspiracies.

Hippie – Day 12

"Why this outfit is a must for any mom"

In nearly one hundred days of blogging about my search for fabulous, no single garment of clothing has garnered as many compliments as the tunic I wore yesterday –

Eight total compliments! The sources ranged from children, to friends, to a stranger ("I like your shirt/dress/whatever that is!"), to my husband, which I'm not totally sure counts because he compliments me all the time. Even when I was two hundred pounds and nine months pregnant he found something nice to say (which at that point is lying, not complimenting). But, hey, I'm adding his compliment to the total anyway.

I got so many compliments that by the end of the day I began talking to people differently. Instead of actually listening to what they had to say, I just stood preoccupied waiting for "tunic talk" to begin. *Yes, yes, yes, you just got out of the hospital, diagnosis not good, probably not going to make it to Halloween... Uh, have you noticed my tunic yet?* I dipped my toe in the water of self-absorption yesterday and I liked it! It reminded me of that Fran Lebowitz quote, "Listening is just waiting to talk." Talk about my tunic, that is...

As for the person who didn't know exactly what my shirt/dress/ whatever actually was, it is called a tunic. I didn't know this either until a few days ago when I researching hippie looks. Tunics were invented in ancient Rome and they have been worn all around the world ever since. My tunic is being delicately washed on cold right now, so that I can wear it again as soon as possible... because once you experience tunic fame, ordinary life is just not as colorful.

Hippie -- Day 19

"The best compliment a mom could ever hear"

A very inexplicable and bizarre encounter happened to me at Starbucks yesterday. After my 3-year-old son, August, and I, placed our order, the friendly, twenty-something barista had this conversation with me:

Barista guy: *(indicating August) So, you got stuck with babysitting duty today, huh?"*

Me: *(confused) "Excuse me?"*

Barista guy: *"That kid is your little brother, right?"*

A long moment of stunned silence from me.

Me: *"No, he's my son."*

Barista guy: *(shocked)* *"Wow, I totally thought he was your little brother."*

As I walked to our table shaking, giddy, confused and wondering how anyone could think I looked young enough to have a 3-year-old for a brother instead of a 3-year-old for a son, I came up with the following possibilities:

1. *Barista guy is blind, but is really good at making eye contact and coffee.*

2. *Barista guy assumed I was young from my spunky, hippie outfit, but that I was afflicted with Progeria, the rapidly aging disease.*

3. *The Starbucks counter is deceptively wide. Instead of the standard two feet, Starbucks employees are actually taking your order from space, hence, the fuzzy visibility.*

4. *Barista guy has a fetish for haggard and distracted grown women and knows exactly what to say to charm the mom jeans right off of them.*

Because, I must say, even in the most flattering of lighting, I would never, ever, under any circumstances be confused with a teenager. And even though I am mocking and dismissing this encounter as complete farce, I definitely know two things - one, my youthful hippie outfit had something to do with this wonderful, age-confusing mistake and therefore I will love, love, LOVE hippie style FOREVER. And secondly, it's a crazy mistake for sure, but it's a mistake that I will never forget.

Chapter 13

Bombshell

I saved Bombshell for last because I didn't want to lose all credibility by telling you that Bombshell is a perfectly acceptable style for most moms. It's not. Sure, there are moms out there that rock the Bombshell/Bettie Page look. They've got the choppy bangs, vintage dresses, cool tattoos and look absolutely fantastic. But for the rest of us, it's a really hard style to pull off. Just the high heels alone would have most of us running in the opposite direction of this style.

But Bombshell is a very important look. Consider it your "In case of a fancy emergency style". A Bombshell outfit is like a super hero suit – always ready to spring into action for that surprise wedding invitation or holiday party. And because it's Bombshell, it never goes out of style! Bombshell is especially important for moms who rock the Slacker or Sporty Chic look because those styles don't really have fancy counterparts, so you need Bombshell to round out your wardrobe.

And besides, Bombshells have more fun. They just do. I didn't believe it either until I tried out Bombshell style. It didn't matter that I don't have a Bombshell body AT ALL. I mean, really, how much padding can one woman stuff into her bra without looking like I have a paper-towel hoarding obsession?

But much to my surprise, Bombshell forgave me for my lack of curves and embraced me as if I had the body of Marilyn Monroe. *I had more men hit on me with this style than any other.* Everywhere I turned there was some guy striking up a conversation with me. It was crazy. And to be perfectly honest, after being married for twelve years and having three kids, it was kind of nice to know that I still have *something going on.* All I had to do was put on Bombshell.

Things you'll need:

1. *Push-up bra* – It's time to hoist those girls up! Get a lacy one and some panties to match. It's against Bombshell laws to wear a sexy bra with giant mom underwear.

2. *Halter-top* – Gotta wear this with a push up bra. Tits ahoy.

3. *Fuzzy angora sweater* – Should hit above your waist, fitted and extra fuzzy.

4. *High-waisted pencil skirt* – A Bombshell pencil skirt is longer, tighter and comes up higher on the waist. Put a big, patent leather vintage belt over it for that sexy secretary look.

5. *Vintage red dress* – Wear it with stilettos and glamorous sunglasses and you'll cause traffic accidents.

6. *Fake fur collared retro sweater* – I'm against buying fur, but sometimes if you're shopping in a vintage store, these old sweaters have real fur. This makes it easier to justify the purchase when you know the animal would have died of old age by now anyway.

7. *Platform Mules* – These shoes can have a fuzzy puffball. I repeat – These shoes can have a fuzzy puffball.

8. *Animal print stilettos* – Bombshells wear animal prints, so in addition to getting some cheetah stilettos, you could also think about a sexy animal print cami or animal print jacket. (Not to be worn all at once, particularly near a zoo.)

9. *Clutch purse* – Bombshells do not carry mom-sized purses. Just another reason why this is a "special occasion" only style.

10. *See-through blouse* – With a cami or just a lacy bra underneath. Your choice.

11. *Brooch* – I like to go for a pure grandma brooch. It adds a little quirkiness to the whole sex goddess thing.

12. *Halter dress* – These can either be very fitted or have big, flowing skirts. Once again, it's all about being boobalicous.

Outfit ideas for fancy occasions:

1. Vintage red dress, animal print stilettos, fake fur collared retro sweater, clutch.

2. Pencil skirt, platform mules, halter-top, push up bra, brooch.

3. Pencil skirt, see through blouse, animal print stilettos, push up bra.

4. Halter dress, platform mules, clutch, push up bra.

5. Pencil skirt, fuzzy angora sweater, halter-top, brooch, stilettos, patent leather vintage belt.

6. Halter dress, animal print stilettos, fake fur collared retro sweater, clutch, push up bra, brooch.

Blog Posts

Bombshell -- Day 7

"Bravery thy name is Bombshell"

Fortunately, because of a successful mall trip today, I have added extensively to my Bombshell *dress collection.* I never go to the mall without my kids so I was thrilled to discover that there are actually stores in the mall other than *Build-a-Bear*. Who knew? In less than an hour, I bought 3 dresses at Banana Republic, 2 pairs of shoes, a belt at Macys and 2 push-up cheetah print bras at Victoria's Secret. I was in a glorious, child-free-Starbucks-fueled consumer haze.

I still need to work on the hair and makeup, which is to say that I need to do something with my hair and *put makeup on*. I loved this dress in the fitting room -- I was like, *Bombshell, meet Holly... Holly, meet Bombshell...* But when I got it home and looked at it against the harsh reality of our goat/pig/dog/child-infested homestead, well, I became slightly terrified and all I could think was... *Am I brave enough to wear this outfit beyond our driveway?*

And the answer is -- I don't think I am -- but I'm going to do it anyway....

Bombshell -- Day 8

"A Bombshell gets comfortable"

I have not worn the red dress beyond my driveway yet, but I promise, there will be an occasion this month where my dress and I will have an adventure. Maybe a date night out with my husband? Maybe Thanksgiving dinner? I know my son has a field trip to the library next week. Why, this dress might be the perfect chaperone outfit! I could even buy some cat's eye granny glasses for that "sexy librarian" look. Or if the mood strikes me, I could pretend *I don't know how to read* and could play a game of trying to coax some random man at the library to read to me.

Today I did what zillions of moms around the world did with their kids today -- ran errands and went to the park. Nothing unusual about my day at all, except, of course, my choice of clothing and shoes –

My candy apple red lipstick arrived from Sephora and I slathered it all over my lips before I left the house, but it had completely worn off by the time this picture was taken. Legend has it that some women put lipstick in their purses and re-apply it throughout the day, but I have to do some more investigating before I actually believe this to be true.

Did I feel overdressed for such banal everyday life events? Why, yes, I did. But did I feel silly? Surprisingly, no. It was actually really fun. *Look at me! I'm in a fancy dress! For no reason!* And if I ever felt my confidence wavering, I would just tell myself -- you might not think you're going anywhere, but you're going *everywhere...*

Bombshell -- Day 14

"A Bombshell sees red"

This is the third and final pencil skirt from my Bombshell shopping spree. It's vintage. It's red. It's linen. And believe it or not, it's actually comfortable.

This outfit is so, "Mr. Peterson, I have the files you requested."

I wore this outfit all day and was just fine with it. No dreams of running home and putting on pajamas. The only downside is that the skirt is so fitted I had to take little baby steps all day -- no striding like a hulking Neanderthal the way I usually do. The only accident that befell my Bombshell outfit today was that one of our goats tore a large hole in my shirt.

Garfield butted me to say hello (a sign of affection in the goat world and reason number 85 on a long list of reasons to avoid getting goats), his horn caught in my shirt and he pulled back so hard that he practically tore my sleeve off. He was really sorry. Actually, he wasn't. (This is reason number 95 to avoid getting goats. They have a staggering lack of remorse.)

It's fine. I think I can sew it, but it will be very unsightly. Just ask my children. Half of their clothes look like the prototypes Dr. Frankenstein made before he settled on the monster.

So that's it as far as my Bombshell shopping spree. I've worn everything except a vintage dress I'm really excited about for Thanksgiving dinner. The rest of this month I'm going to have to work on mixing and matching different outfits together -- a skill I find akin to rocket science. I can't believe I'm saying this, but I'm a little sad that my Bombshell month has gone by so fast. It turned out to be so much more fun than I expected. I highly encourage you to try it... Just see how you feel in it. You might surprise yourself.

Bombshell -- Day 22

"The best Bombshell outfit ever"

I've been doing this fashion experiment for 319 days so far and yesterday's outfit earned the *most compliments* of any outfit I've worn this entire year....

Why am I being photographed in a bathroom? I'll explain that later. First, I'd like to share *all the compliments*. I'm also going to write them down in permanent marker, put them in a time capsule and bury them in our yard for future generations and mutant cockroaches to enjoy in the year 3000.

THE COMPLIMENTS –

"You look hot." (From a mom at school)

"You look soooo hot." (From my children's art teacher)

"You look really hot." (From a man who approached me at the grocery store. This was the only compliment of the day that I didn't really enjoy. He then went on to say, "You know what's the best part about your heels? You get to be taller than guys like me." This confused me. Why is that the best part about my heels, small man? I would have asked him, but did not want to prolong the conversation.)

This was a banner day for me. I don't think I've gotten "three hots" in one day ever. I'm actually not sure I've ever ever gotten one hot in a day from, you know, someone other than my husband. But did the compliments stop there? Oh no, they just got specific.

"I love your skirt." (Woman passing me on the street.)

"I love your skirt." (Another woman passing me on the street like ten seconds later.)

"I love, love, love your skirt. Like so much I want to steal it." (From another woman passing me on the street. My kids thought this was the funniest compliment of the day.)

"I love your shoes!" (From yet another woman.)

Then, the icing on the compliment cake. A woman walked past me while I was at the park and said, "You're looking very Bombshell today." She then smiled and said she liked my blog. That made my day!

Now, the reason I took a picture of my *most complimented outfit ever* in a public bathroom is simple – I was so delirious with praise that I almost forgot to take a picture at all. My kids and I went to see a pirate show last night and as we were using the bathroom before the show I realized that I had not documented the outfit!

My day yesterday really proves to me the power of fashion. My entire experience was affected by what I was wearing. I was the same person, walking around the same town, and yet everything was different. Amazing. I mean, really, we're just talking about clothes here.

Bombshell -- Day 30

"Confessions of a Bombshell"

    I cannot actually believe that my Bombshell month is already over. Since the start of "My Year of Fabulous", I have dreaded the possibility of having a Bombshell month and now look at me -- on the other side of this dreaded look already.

    And you know what? *It wasn't dreaded at all!*

    Bombshell was fun. Really fun. And so liberating! When you make yourself wear really dressy clothes when *no one else around you is dressy*, something inside of you changes. First, you realize that you've actually been trying to fit in with the people around you even if you were doing it subconsciously. Then you realize that it's kind of silly to try and fit in with the people around you. I mean, they're them and you're you -- and that's a good thing. Life is more interesting that way.

    It's just like Dr. Seuss says --

    "I am I! And I may not know why but I know that I like it! Three cheers! I am I!"

    Is Bombshell my permanent style? *Of course not.* But I learned that Bombshell is great for special occasions. I never have to fear/wonder what to wear to another wedding again. I can dress up for Christmas, Easter, even Groundhog Day. There is no occasion Bombshell can't make more festive.

I mean, why go to the mall and get some "just okay" dress when you can go to a vintage store and buy some spectacular? Something that's so well made? Something that's timeless.

Out of all my styles this year, I'm keeping a lot of my Bombshell clothes. They're in my closet just waiting for me to put them on to do something special.

Chapter 14

The Three B's: Buying, Budget and Butts

This chapter is all about taking what you've learned so far and putting it into action. It's time for you to start *buying*. And the only way to really know if a style is right for you is to wear it every single day for a week. I know what you're thinking, "She wants me to buy a *week's* worth of clothes just to *see* if I like a style? Oh well, I guess my children can go without food for a week. It's all in the name of fashion!"

This brings me to *budget*. You are not allowed to spend more than *two hundred dollars* on an entire week's worth of clothes. Your style trial week is not about buying a Burberry trench coat if you *think* you might be Gamine. Your style trial is about finding the least expensive versions of everything you might want and seeing how you feel in them. This can be done at thrift stores, consignment stores, online consignment stores like Thredup.com or even just raiding your friends' closets. If you discover a style that you really love, great, you can start accumulating all the Cartier tank watches you want. If not, you have a couple hundred dollars worth of clothes that you can take to a consignment store or re-sell online and recoup some of your money. The clothes you don't sell can be re-gifted to a distant relative or unaware, similarly-sized friend.

Another really fun way of discovering your look is to make it a team effort. Gather ten friends together, have each one pick a style and try it out for a week, then rotate. Obviously, unless you hang out only with people that are your exact size, then you're going to have to make some adjustments along the way. But you'll still save money and, even better, get the moral support you need and have a blast while figuring out your style. (You don't have to do this with ten friends. Three or four friends or just your BFF works great too.)

But before you do any of this, I'd like to talk about the final "B" of this chapter -- *butts*. I want you to really hear what I'm about to say because it's the most important piece of advice I have in this book.

Do not wait to find your style until you finally have the body you dream of having someday.

This type of thinking can keep you trapped on Ugly Mom Island forever. I'm not saying that you're never going to get in shape so you might as well give up and wear a feed sack around all day. What I'm saying is that you need to start looking and feeling better *today* – whether you have buns of steel or not.

Embrace your style regardless of how you feel about your body today. Trust me, you'll feel better instantly. You'll get tons of compliments and your self-esteem will start coming back to life the moment you start paying attention to you again.

Chapter 15

The Ten Commandments of Mom Fashion

1. Accept your body as it is today.

Buying great clothes for your *current body* does not mean you are giving up on your *imagined future body*. It only means you've made a decision to look fantastic during the transition.

2. Never buy anything new.

Children have an amazing knack for seeking out your most treasured fashion possession and barfing on it or sneezing in it or wiping it with Cheetos fingers. Avoid this frustration entirely by wearing used clothing. During my last trip to Goodwill, I scored a pair of Vera Wang boyfriend jeans for *five dollars*. The first time I wore them I accidentally sat on a mound of play dough and I didn't even get upset. *Thank you, five-dollar jeans.* You not only make me look great, but you keep "evil mommy" from appearing.

3. Never wear big white sneakers.

It's really the jeans and sneaker combination that gives moms such a bad fashion reputation. What, are we all running 5K's in our Lady Wranglers? But stylish, cute and comfortable shoes are everywhere now. There's no reason we have to continue to wear sneakers that can be seen from space.

4. Never wear a kid's backpack.

If you're wearing something that could hang on a hook outside a fifth grade classroom, something is terribly wrong.

5. Pick a style.

And tell the world who you are.

6. Go to school on jeans.

Try on as many styles and as many different designers you can get your hands on. Finding that perfect pair of jeans is like finding a good bathing suit – a painful, harrowing experience that may lead to you rocking back and forth, face in hands, in the corner of a dressing room. But when you find that perfect pair of jeans that looks good at every angle, it will *all feel worth it.*

7. Don't wear a ponytail unless you're exercising or sick.

There's no point in having long hair if it's always up in a ponytail. It doesn't scream youthful, it screams lazy. Get a cute haircut. If you hate it, it will grow out. That's the beauty of hair!

8. Never compare yourself to a celebrity mom.

The *average awesome mom* is not the same as the celebrity mom. If we were the same then we'd all get tummy tucks at the same time we had our "emergency C-sections" and we'd all have personal chefs making us delicious, yet calorie conscious post-partum meals at home while our hot, metro-sexual personal trainer massaged the cellulite off our legs like some kind of Kobe cow. I don't know if the celebrity mom will ever pull back the curtain and reveal the entourage that keeps her looking like so *not a mommy,* but nonetheless, we need to stop comparing ourselves to her and start acknowledging the differences between our two species.

9. Get support.

We can't minimize this problem. Changing your clothes isn't as easy as well, changing your clothes. It's an emotional process and we need the help of friends to get through it.

10. Wear a dress once a week.

Forcing yourself to wear a dress once a week is like checking in with your fashion parole officer. It will remind you not to slip back into your old sweatpants ways. Sure, it's a pain to get the whole outfit together (The shoes! The belt! The jewelry!), but once you do, it's so empowering. You will burst out your front door and announce, "Hello, everyone! I'm off to nowhere in particular.... in a dress!"

Buddha says...

"What you are is what you have been. What you'll be is what you do now."

Chapter 16

The New You

Are you excited? Are you nervous? Are you nauseous? That's okay. It's one thing to read about something you want to do, but to put it into practice, well, that's another thing entirely. It's almost like giving birth. So much preparation – all the books, all the classes, all the deep breathing and meditation and then the first big labor pain hits and you think, *All right, this is horrible. I'm going home.*

In a way, you are giving birth again – but this time to a whole new you. And there are times when it's going be painful – you'll wear something that looks totally stupid on you and you'll want to give up. Or you won't have the right belt or shirt or the time or energy to try to look runway ready just to take your kid to the dentist. Don't give up. Learning is all about making mistakes. Do you ever expect your kids to do something perfectly the first time they try something? Of course not. Gosh Timmy, your Dad and I got you this bicycle assuming you could ride it in the Tour de France next week. Why do you keep falling over?

When it comes to fashion, give yourself the same amount of patience you give your children when they learn something new. Don't expect to get it right the first time. Give yourself time to fall over. And if you just keep trying you will figure it out. I promise.

You can do this. You are beautiful. Now go show the world.

www.ingramcontent.com/pod-product-compliance
Lightning Source LLC
Chambersburg PA
CBHW060150300526
45790CB00014B/397